GOPALA

THE RASA LILA

Swamini Sri Lalitambika Devi

ISBN 978-0-9960236-8-9

TABLE OF CONTENTS

FOREWORD

TO EMBRACE THE PLAY OF LIFE is to awaken. We live the drama each day—

We seek the truth of the Lord. We glimpse the Lord, and then we fall out of the Lord's presence, into the angst and sorrow of worldly *roga*.

We seek and find and lose again, until the sun rises on that blessed morning when the mind is pure and the heart true, such that we become ever one with the divine beloved.

Just as the play of life unfolds, so too is this tale of the *rasa lila* revealed to us as a play within a play, with the tales of Sri Krisna's childhood staged amid the greater story of divine longing.

One autumn night, the *gopis* leave their homes and families for the call of the Lord's flute, only to find themselves alone by the moonlit river. As they long for the cherished companionship of their youthful cowherd Lord, the *gopis* re-enact his heroic antics.

Their devotional play reminds us to guard against the tricks and trials of daily life—the enchantment of worldly pleasure; the ceremonial dogma of religion; the treachery of false friends; and the emotive distractions of our own minds, the anger, desire, and pride.

These scenes of divine childhood also cue us to nourish the innate virtues of the heart—piety, charity, discernment, tenderness, and gratitude—so that we may awaken to the eternal presence of the divine beloved.

Truly, the Lord does not come and go. Where could the Lord go? The Lord is ever-present.

It is we who fall out of the presence, when we forget to attend to the heart.

Childish and fickle in our love, our attention is attracted time and time again by the elations and sorrows of the world, the mind's ebb and flow of emotion, and even the intricacies of intellect.

So, the Lord disappears from time to time, to rouse a more constant devotion in our hearts.

We need not grieve at this apparent disappearance, for we who would awaken from the play of the world through the Lord's grace pray with fervent devotion:

Lord, you live forever in the heart.
Forgive us our failings.

Bless us with the grace of purity
in divine love, beyond time

and space. May all beings of earth,
water, sky, and space rejoice in you.

So, may all beings be liberated
in the eternal presence of divine love.

I
LONGING

THE GOPIS DANCED as if they had drunk barrels of wine. Around and around they spun, the balls of their feet sinking into the damp earth of the riverbank. All the while, they laughed and sang.

Their faces opened like the white lotus flowers that bloomed upon the moonlit waters. Their glances were coy and their arms graceful. Their laughter rivaled the tinkling bells of their anklets, ringing out into the night.

They had arrived at the riverbank suddenly, some with *kohl* drawn across one eyelid, others wearing no more than their underskirts. Earrings swung wildly, and cheeks were flushed.

Each of the *gopis* had dropped whatever she was doing upon hearing the first notes of his flute rise through the night. Some left home while they had been milking the cows or suckling their infants. Others abandoned the hearthfire with the cakes yet baking, the milk steaming.

Now, they stood together, gathered at the river. The moon rose overhead like the full face of a yearning lover. The lotus blossoms floating upon the water opened wide eyes to the moon.

This was an autumn night, so the moon glowed red as saffron, and yet jasmine bloomed with abandon—though that flower favors the tender months of spring and summer.

On the banks of the river stood the boy, crowned with a plume of peacock feathers. He played a simple song upon his flute, as if he had not a care in the world. Golden flowers dangled from his ears, while lotus blossoms wreathed his neck like a garland of victory.

This boy had lived for all his life in the rural village that flourished along the banks of the river, a dairy town where the people tended cows and sold milk, butter, and cheese at market for a living; yet he was like no other boy of the countryside. Young as he was, he herded the cows with the mature dignity of a sage, even as his mirthful pranks and sweet songs endeared him to the villagers. He was a favorite companion to the *gopis*, who had this very night come running from the village to meet him at the riverbanks.

Indeed, this boy was no ordinary lad, but a child of noble blood. Although no one spoke of his birthright, his uncle was king of the land just east of the river.

Yes, his mother's brother was a powerful sovereign, such that when she had married, her dowry included two hundred ladies-in-waiting, four hundred gold-decked elephants, fifteen thousand horses, and one thousand eight hundred carriages.

The king himself had taken the reins of the carriage, in which the bride and groom were seated, and led the elaborate wedding procession.

Well-wishers thronged along the road, singing and playing musical instruments. They jostled one another in their exuberant efforts to catch a glimpse of the royal procession.

The king acknowledged his subjects now and again with gracious nods to the right and to the left, when suddenly he heard a voice rise from the crowd. The king scanned the mob, his eyes narrow with determination, yet who had spoken he could not tell. Even so, amid the joyful sounds of conch and kettle drum, the words were clear, a dire prophecy: The eighth child of these newlyweds would slay him.

The king shuddered. Long had he feared losing power over the fertile land he ruled, for he had indeed usurped the throne unlawfully from his own father. No good could come to one such as he who overthrows a parent, the father who had kindly raised him with every pleasure and advantage.

Seated in the chariot, the newly married couple gazed at each other, their eyes wide with confusion and wonder at the prophecy.

The celebration continued, though the king no longer rejoiced; and yet, the dire prediction intoned by a mysterious stranger brought neither humility nor repentance to his cold heart. As he held the reins of the wedding carriage, he quietly resolved to save himself by putting his newly married sister to death before her wedding night.

He jerked at the reins, startling the horses and bringing the wedding festivities to a sudden halt. Then, he turned and seized his sister by the hair. His brow was fierce and his hands determined, as he unsheathed his sword.

The crowd surged, rising up to see what ceremonial delight had brought the parade to a standstill. Trumpets blared, as the crowd clamored, yet held back by the king's entourage.

The girl gazed up at her fierce brother, her eyes wide with fear. Was her life to end on this day that ought to have been filled with joy and new beginnings? She was as innocent and helpless as a doll in her brother's impassioned hands.

The girl's husband sought to calm the king with reason.

"Your highness, murdering your sister will only enslave you to sin," he said. "Think of your own welfare, if not of hers."

This mode of persuasion elicited no response from the unlawful king, who continued to brandish his sword. His greatest desire was to hold the throne. He had already jailed his father to usurp the crown and had no qualms about committing murder to retain his power. He held his sister fast by the hair and raised the sword even higher. Sunlight glinted from the narrow blade.

The girl's husband persisted, desperate to save her. "We will give you every one of our children," he promised. "You may do as you like with them. In this way, you may guard your life against the prophecy. Only let my wife live."

The tyrant considered this offer. His first priority was to guard his life and right to the throne. He did wish his sister well, so long as her prosperity did not threaten his. His brow furrowed, and the sword came to rest at this side. Were he to kill every one of his sister's children, then the eighth could not slay him as prophesied. This logic seemed definitive.

He did not consider slaying the infants as murder so much as the rightful protection of his throne. His brow contorted with indecision, but he finally agreed. Yes, he might yet spare his sister's life on her wedding day.

And so, he released the terrified girl.

Taking his wife into his arms, the husband bowed in gratitude to the tyrant, yet his chest felt hollow, his thudding heart torn asunder at the thought of relinquishing his every child to death at the hands of the corrupt monarch.

The king lifted the reins of the carriage and whipped the horses. So, the wedding procession continued down the road, as the crowd cheered.

The sounds of kettle drum and conch were jubilant, and the gold-trimmed carriages glinted in the sunlight. Even so, the afternoon shadows had begun to lengthen.

II

Disappearance

As promised, each child was given at birth to the unlawful monarch, who was their uncle. He slew the first seven infants without remorse, for fear of losing the throne and his life.

The eighth child, the one truly prophesied to slay the king, was born at midnight. His birth was like a sunrise in the dark of night.

The young mother swaddled her infant in precious golden silks.

If this newborn were relinquished to his ruling uncle as had been the first seven, he would be put to death before the sun set the next evening; yet surely, the prophecy given on their wedding day was divine and meant to be fulfilled. The child must be saved. They would break their promise to her brother. She cooed to the child for a moment and then pressed him into his father's arms.

Her husband took the treasured infant and hastened far from the royal palace, along the road and out of the city. Rain lashed the rivers. Thunder rolled, as lightning cracked the sky.

The child's father held him close, keeping the blessed newborn warm and dry, as he made his way to a nearby village. There, he knew of an esteemed cowherd whose wife had recently given birth. This cowherd was a village leader who could raise his eighth son with every advantage. Moreover, no one would think to search a rustic hamlet for a child of royal lineage. There, the boy would be safe and live to slay the king, liberating people far and wide from tyranny.

So, he left his newborn son in the care of this cowherd family, while they slept.

When the sun rose the next morning, the cowherd and his wife took the foster infant to be their own. They did not notice that the boy's rightful father had taken their newborn in exchange, to be offered at the hands of the bloodthirsty king. They rejoiced in the laughter and antics of the delightful infant, whom they presumed to be theirs.

In this way, the boy's life was spared, and he of noble birth was raised in a small, rural village.

As the boy matured, he became known throughout the village for the music of his flute, which he played such that all grief was dispelled. So sweet were the melodies of his flute that the village *gopis* flocked to him. They felt themselves relieved of all worldly distress in his serene presence.

Now, by the river on this autumn night, the boy stood beneath the full harvest moon, his skin more luminous than the golden silk *dhoti* he wore. He posed like a dancer, with ankles crossed and the toes of one foot poised upon the fertile earth. He was delighted by the fragrance of jasmine, which bloomed in starry abundance along the riverbanks. His face radiant, he wooed the *gopis* with each languorous note.

Yet hidden amid the foliage, the *gopis* gathered in flushed disarray. The ringing of their delicate ankle bells harmonized with the irresistible melodies of the boy's flute, as they straightened their skirts and wove flowers through their hair. Caught up in this sweet music of the night, they forgot all responsibility to home and hearth. They burst forth suddenly from the copse of slender trees onto the riverbank, where he stood.

Ever the merry prankster, the boy feigned surprise at their arrival.

"What brings you into the forest so late, tonight?" he asked, ever child-like. "Wild beasts may crouch in the bushes, and your families are sure to miss you. Please, don't worry your loved ones."

The *gopis* gazed in wonder upon the boy. His curls were long and black, and his complexion dark yet luminous. His face outshone the moon.

The boy continued to jest with abandon. "Ah! You must have come to gather the moonlit flowers, to watch light play across the waters."

The *gopis* stood, breathless. Did he not know the depth of their love for him?

The boy smiled brightly. "So now, you have enjoyed this fragrant night. At home, your children and calves are crying to be fed. Return to them."

Still, the *gopis* remained before him on the riverbank, their hearts pounding from having run so quickly to meet him.

The boy continued, elaborating upon the charade. "What? Have you come to see me?" He shook his head with mock concern. "A married woman must not think of another, or her reputation will be tarnished. Stay true to your husbands, children, and parents. Do not stray from your familial duties out of longing for a simple lad like me."

At this point, the milkmaid's youthful faces revealed their heightening distress. How could their beloved *gopala* reject them like this, when they would give up everything in the world for love of him?

Noting their dismay, the boy acquiesced. "Well, if you must, then think of me, speak of me, and sing of me—as you perform your necessary household duties."

The *gopis* gasped.

"Yes, let your love for me be chaste. Go home," he admonished playfully. Then, he turned, seemingly unconcerned that they had abandoned all they cared for most to dance with him on this moonlit night.

The *gopis* stood, lost in confusion. They had run this night to the riverbank in answer to the call of the boy's melodious flute. Truly, he brought joy to their hearts as nothing else in the village did, not even their husbands or children. Now, they stood despondent, their lips dry with disappointed sighs.

One of the *gopis* was so disconcerted that she began to twist a lock of her hair, disheveling the jasmine blossoms she had woven through the tresses. The starry petals scattered across the ground.

Another beseeched him directly, "Please, do not send us away."

Then, they all chimed in, and their voices sounded like the ringing of many bells. "You speak of duty and family life, but we will not turn back. Our daily chores bring no joy compared with time spent at your feet. What virtue do we gain in wasting our days and nights by the hearth fire?"

The boy's head cocked, as he listened intently, and so they continued with deepening fervor.

"Saints renounce the passing distractions of worldly life and think only of what is true. We are not learned in scripture or ritual, yet we do know that you mean everything to us. Your words are like nectar. You are the jewel of this village. Simple boy, just the ringing of your anklets causes us to forget everything of the world, pain and pleasure alike."

He did not again insist that they leave him, and so their voices rose with hope.

"In abandoning our families for you, our souls will be liberated. We follow in the footsteps of the wise, leaving behind the passing sorrows and joys of mundane village life for the divine radiance, which we find in you."

The boy sighed. Child though he was, he knew that these *gopis* were not to abandon their families as had the ascetic masters. Even so, he wished that they might know the truth of divine love, for he was indeed delighted by their intentions, by their devotional eloquence.

He grinned, and bowed to them, ever debonair in his youthful grace.

The *gopis* received this courtly gesture as an invitation to remain with him by the river that night. Their faces lit up the glen.

Now, the boy lifted the small wooden flute to his lips and played a tune simple and sweet as if he were a *gandharva*, bringing their feet to dance, and then he began to sing. His child-like hands stroked their hair and pressed up against their fingertips.

The river rippled in time with their dance. White lotus blossoms shone from the waters.

In the flowering trees, birds began to sing, mistaking midnight for dawn.

The *gopis* were elated.

As the *gopis* danced and danced, each became convinced that the boy dallied only with her. Their tender hearts began to heave and swell with pride above the swirl of their colorful peasant frocks.

Not one said a word to the others, but each reveled in the thought, "This boy must love me, alone."

And so, the *gopis* twirled about on the banks of the river, each delighted to be the boy's chosen favorite, until looking up, they realized one by one that their beloved *gopala* had disappeared into the dark of night.

III

THE PLAY

LIKE A HERD OF ELEPHANT COWS who have lost their bull, the *gopis* became deranged. They were mad with grief at the boy's disappearance. His smile, his glance, his voice, and his sport had captivated them, so that they could think of nothing else.

In a moment of ecstatic lunacy, each of the *gopis* began to imagine that she indeed was the boy, declaring to the moon, "I am he," and then longing for him, again.

Together, they roamed through the forest asking of the trees where the boy had gone. They beseeched the limbs of fig, mango, and jackfruit. They interrogated the trunk of wood-apple and the leaves of basil.

Finally, they cried out into the night, offering their most tender endearments, in the hope that he might hear but one fond name that pleased him and return to them.

Where was he, so sweet like honey that the humming black bees swarmed after him?

As they walked, they felt young grass shoots erect with longing beneath their feet. They knelt and praised the earth that had been so recently graced by the brief touch of his soles.

They continued to roam through the forest in search of their lost *gopala*, and so they happened upon a doe, whom he had blessed in passing. Her lustrous eyes were yet wide with the sight of his face and the sound of his flute. In her gaze, they became as gentle as she was.

Flowering vines clung with grace to the tree trunks, as they *gopis* imagined they would to the boy, should he appear again. A fragrant breeze wafted through the forest, and the looping tendrils shivered with delight.

Still, the boy did not appear. He seemed to have vanished into the night.

At length, the *gopis* began to tire, for the search seemed futile. The boy could not be found. Reluctantly, they abandoned their wanderings.

Now, sadly resigned to his absence, they began to mime his antics. One made a game of calling the cows, while another pretended to play an invisible flute; yet, however delicate the fair *gopis* were, they appeared clumsy in imitating the boy.

Still yearning for him, they decided to re-enact the scenes of his early feats. They took on various roles, casting themselves as wicked enchantress, rickety milkcart, mighty whirlwind, distraught mother, demon calf, monstrous crane, venomous serpent, blazing wildfire, disastrous flood, cowherd comrades, simple villagers, wicked king, and each in turn the beloved boy himself.

And so, that autumn night, the *gopis* began to frolic, reliving their favorite moments of the boy's life, until the leafy glen again rang with their cries and laughter. The forest floor became a stage, strewn with jasmine and mimosa blossoms. The curtain of the night lifted and, lit by the full moon that glowed red as saffron, the play began.

Scene I
The Enchantress

THE WICKED KING HAD SPARED the life of his sister on her wedding day, and now he awaited the birth of her eighth child, whom the strange voice in the procession had prophesied would slay him.

He slew the eight newborns relinquished to him, but yet suspected that the divine infant lived. He suffered with night terrors and insomnia when he lay down to sleep at night, and he brooded incessantly over the matter by day.

His sister and her husband could not possibly be raising this eighth infant themselves, he reasoned. There would be no way to hide their child, for his ministers patrolled the streets and he had gifts delivered regularly to their home.

He was convinced that the nursling must yet live elsewhere, disguised as the descendant of another bloodline. Finally, the king could stand his panic no longer. He determined to have the neighboring farmlands searched.

Were he to travel through the countryside himself, a caravan of ministers would accompany him, an entourage which would bring him immediate recognition. So, the king plotted to send someone else in his place—a woman.

The woman whom he engaged for this purpose was a gypsy with broad knowledge of herbs and incantations. Unlike true healers, her use of such medicinals was not always benevolent. For this very reason, the scheming king confided in her, trusting the treacherous witch with his secret suspicions about the auspicious child.

The gypsy was amenable to the king's wishes. Her art was not that of healing but of deluding and destroying. She used her powers to fulfill selfish ends, profiting from the reckless fears and desires of those around her. Her heart was like that of a viper.

And so, between the king and the gypsy, an evil plot was hatched. The gypsy was to seek out the newly born of the neighboring villages and suckle them as if she were a wet nurse; however, her nipples would be smeared with poison. Every child who drank the milk of her bosom was sure to die.

In his raging paranoia, the king had no qualms about killing all male infants of the countryside. Among the many innocents slain, he reasoned, would be his infant nemesis. The death of this prophesied child would surely leave him safe to rule the prosperous cities west of the river.

The gypsy acceded with gracious deference to the king's wishes. She was giddy with delight at the prospect of ingratiating herself with the crown.

She prepared carefully for her mission, so that the simple village folk might trust her as the king had. She dressed her hair with fragrant jasmine and adorned her ears with golden hoops. Gazing into the mirror, she practiced an ingratiating smile sure to endear her to the cowherds and their wives. Finally, through trickery, she became divinely beautiful, her skin smooth and supple, her eyes lustrous, her cheeks abloom, and her lips succulent.

She could not change her heart, which was dark with the poisons of ignorance, anger, and greed, but no matter. The benevolent villagers welcomed this gypsy, as if she were good fortune herself.

The beautiful sorceress soon became popular at local gatherings. She received countless invitations to dine with the cowherds and their families. In her guile, she was careful to pose no threat to the women of the village, maintaining perfect chastity along with her enchanting decorum.

Meanwhile, she took a careful interest in the village children, watching their games with admiration, offering them handfuls of milk-sweets and pieces of ripe fruit. A shrewd observer, she quickly recognized the child prophesied to overthrow the wicked king, his uncle.

The boy was impossible to overlook, luminous in complexion and adorned with golden silks as he was. His foster parents were among the wealthiest of the village, his father a leader of the cowherds. The family stabled a large herd of animals and employed several servants.

One afternoon, the gypsy knocked at the door of their rustic home, which stood in a quiet hamlet surrounded by private gardens. When the door opened to her, she admired the jasmine that bloomed in the yard and noted the extraordinary size of the mangoes ripening on the trees, their fruit the color of the setting sun amid the thick foliage.

The boy's foster mother was hospitable. She often hosted parties for the villagers and welcomed guests regularly for lunch or weekend visits. She greeted the this traveling gypsy with her characteristic warmth.

As the good woman hastened to the kitchen for the sweet milk-cakes that had brought her renown as a hostess, the gypsy quietly searched the room.

She found the boy napping in a basket. Certainly, he was a delight to behold, illuminating the alcove in which he slept. What a shame that she had been commissioned to put an end to him, yet at the thought of the king's favor, a sly grin spread across her painted lips.

The boy's mother returned bearing a tray piled high with warm milk cakes for her guest, but the gypsy could not take her eyes off of the boy. She nibbled politely at one of the milk cakes and pronounced it delicious, and then bursting with eagerness to fulfill her mission, she begged to hold the infant.

The boy's mother was flattered that this newcomer should immediately attend to her infant, yet she smelled a strange herbal fragrance in the air. She wondered of the gypsy's origins and hesitated.

The gypsy smiled even more sweetly.

"He is the most adorable child I've ever beheld. I long only to caress him. Surely, no harm could come to him in my arms," she said, with a sidelong glance at the child.

All of the villagers doted upon the boy, with his delicate curls and dimples. How natural that this gypsy should want to hold him, thought his mother. Still, she did not acquiesce.

The gypsy struggled with her impatience, as if reining in horses.

The boy's mother frowned. So many in the village had already welcomed this newcomer that she did not want to be rude in questioning her origins. Still, maternal concern tugged at her heart.

The gypsy slowly lowered her eyes, turning away as if fatally disappointed. A tinge of anger began to color her cheeks.

At this, the boy's mother reminded herself of her social obligations as a hostess. The words her mother had taught her arose in her mind—*atithi devo bhava.* Yes, one must welcome a guest as the Lord. Her husband would be displeased with her, if he were to return home and find that she had snubbed this visitor. She must fulfill not only her social obligations but also the religious tenets. And yet, where was the line between honoring the guest as divine and protecting her child?

She glanced down at her serene boy, who seemed to harbor no worries. She swallowed several times, attempting to moisten her throat that she might speak, and offered the gypsy another cake, but the exotic guest was to be forestalled no longer.

"The boy," she said, holding out her arms with dramatic insistence.

The boy's mother smiled, yet feeling a chill in the waning afternoon light. Surely, no harm could come of allowing this guest to hold her child for a moment. She did not want to seem selfish or over-protective. As graciously as she could, she lifted her contented infant from his nap and laid him in the gypsy's robust arms.

The gypsy gazed down at the infant with a satisfied smile. She rocked him in the crook of her left elbow, holding him carefully so that his head did not wobble.

Then, she let her loosened bodice slip.

The boy's mother stiffened. Was this strange woman now to suckle her child? She felt a strong urge to resist, and yet the gypsy silenced her with a defiant glance. She pressed the boy's face to her warm flesh, and he began to suckle without hesitation, holding fast to the poison-smeared nipple.

The gypsy sighed with pleasure, suppressing a raucous cackle of triumph. The infant would die in her arms, and the king would reward her well she was certain, perhaps with extravagant jewelry, acres of land, or even political power. She imagined holding a scepter and ruling at his side, for he might crown her his most favored queen, once he saw how capably she fulfilled his royal wishes.

And then, her throat constricted, as if the room had become airless. The gypsy glanced about, her eyes rolling wildly.

Earlier in the day, the windows had been flung open, and a gentle breeze wafted through the room, yet she continued to gasp for air.

The boy lay radiant in her arms, peaceably nursing. He had latched onto her breast, yet the deadly poison had no effect upon him. On the contrary, he now sucked not only the milk but the very life out of her, she the noxious mother, the disease of infants too weak to survive.

The boy's mother gazed on the scene, a hand clasped to her mouth, unable to move or speak.

The gypsy struggled and gasped, but the infant would not release her. He continued to suck as she weakened, choked, and finally fell down dead on the cottage floor.

With the impact of her fall, fig, mango, and rose-apple trees turned to dust for miles around.

The boy's mother was horrified. She lifted her infant from the gypsy's lifeless arms.

Why had she not listened to her motherly intuition? Now, she clutched the boy to her bosom, as tears washed over her cheeks onto his.

Light shone through the cottage windows, illuminating the dead witch, her breasts now grey and withered. Yet, in spite of her ill intentions, this lost woman had spent her last days in search of the sanctified child, and she had found him. The selfish delusions by which she had lived no longer mattered.

Evil as she had been during her life, her inert form was fragrant, like a heap of jasmine blossoms. She had been liberated from all ignorant treachery by the boy, and the light of her soul ascended.

Scene II
The Fallen Cart

WHEN NEWS OF HIS GYPSY emissary's death reached the city, the king froze with terror. He could not fathom how any infant could overcome such a treacherous witch. He knew that the one who had suckled her to death must be the divinely prophesied child, and that this child was far more powerful than he had imagined.

The king sat ruminating alone in his council-room, late into the night. He must send another mercenary soul to accomplish the deed, but he did not yet know whom. If this second attempt on the child's life were to fail, the foster parents might intuit his royal scheme and forbid newcomers to visit the boy. The next attempt must succeed, stealthily.

In the village just fourteen kilometers east of the king's wealthy realm, the infant's foster parents rejoiced. Their child was three months old.

According to traditional rite, the pious couple prepared to consecrate him to the Lord. They invited *pujaris* from the small temples that dotted the hillside to visit their home. Friends and neighbors gathered to celebrate the child as well, and the flowering gardens were filled with good cheer.

Great preparation was made for the ceremony. The boy's mother and her friends bathed the infant with rosewater, drying him carefully in a soft towel, and anointing him with sandalwood paste and *kumkum*, as if he were a temple *murti* come to life.

Meanwhile, his father strode off with several eminent cowherds to select the finest animals from the stables, those that were young and strong and gave generously of their milk.

The men returned in high spirits and offered the chosen animals to the *pujaris* in attendance, along with cloth, flowers, and incense.

Only after the boy had been washed and the appropriate offerings made did his foster parents present their child, that the ceremony might begin.

The *pujaris* performed the sacred rites with reverence, sending clouds of fragrant incense up into the skies, chanting *mantras* so resonant that their prayers could be heard throughout the village.

The child abided with dignity throughout the ceremony, though finally his head lolled, for he wanted to sleep.

When the ceremony concluded, the boy's mother handed him over to a trusted maid, for the good woman was yet caught up in hosting the festivities in his honor.

"Lay him to sleep in the side-yard. There, we can yet keep an eye on him or hear him if he cries," she said.

The maid did as she was asked, carrying the child out into the yard, where the festivities could be heard only faintly. She placed him carefully swaddled beneath a large cart used to transport milk pitchers to market. She smiled down upon the child, for she loved him as if he had been her own. Yes, here he would sleep shaded and protected, as the festivities continued with growing fervor in the gardens.

Certain of the child's safety, the maid quickly returned to the house to serve milk cakes to the guests.

In the lush gardens, musicians sang folk songs, accompanied by small drums and bells in the hands of devout guests. Other villagers chattered, laughed, and danced in honor of the child, who lay asleep beneath the cart in the side yard.

The boy awoke unattended, after an hour's nap. He found the shade of the cartbed pleasant and gazed in wonder at the pattern of the wooden slats above him, but he was hungry. Sucking his thumb did no good. He longed for his mother's milk. He kicked, thumping his feet against the cartbed, as if it were a drum. So, he joined in with the musical festivities, though none of the guests who had arrived in his honor noticed.

Only the king's new emissary paid him heed.

This spirit of the air had flown that day from the bustling city where the king ruled to this idyllic countryside. Now, he circled slowly, taking in an aerial view of the village, as he searched for the infant.

Even beneath the cart that glinted with steel milk pitchers, the boy's radiance was mesmerizing. The spirit soon caught sight of him.

The sky darkened as the wicked one descended.

Now, the demon swooped in low for a closer look and found that the infant lay quite alone, his feet thumping against the wooden cartbed.

The wily spirit was determined not to fail the king as had the gypsy. He knew that he maintained one advantage over the treacherous woman: He was a shape-shifter. Because he was a spirit, he could take any material form he liked.

Now, he considered what form best to take, to destroy this boy who had been prophesied to slay the king.

The boy lay unprotected in the courtyard, and yet his family and friends, as well as the village priests, were gathered in the nearby garden. Anyone might wander into the yard and notice an intruder. The boy might even wail and call his mother to him.

Finally, this spirit of the air determined to take the form of the cart beneath which the child lay. In the form of the cart, he might deliberately crush the boy, without drawing attention to himself, until the deed was done.

He hovered over the yard like a dank fog.

Beneath the cart, the child was hungry yet for his mother's milk. He sucked at one finger and then another, to no avail. He kicked harder at the wooden planks above him.

Noiselessly, the spirit alighted. He spread himself throughout the cart, infusing the wooden planks, the graceful bow, and even the wheel spokes. Then, he willed with all his might that the cart crush the boy.

The cart remained intact, as the spirit took the blows of the boy's blessed feet like kicks to the stomach.

The spirit cursed the boy and wished harder that the wooden cart would fall and crush the child. Indeed, his bitter malevolence began to rot the wood of the sturdy cart.

As the spirit had hoped, nobody at the gathering noticed the child's plight—not his parents, not the villagers, and not the priests.

They continued to celebrate him in the lush gardens, completely unaware of his welfare. A flute player improvised a lively *raga* and the crowd began to dance, thumping their feet against the earth, the ladies' silver anklets jangling in time with the music. No one thought to check on the boy, whom they assumed was safely napping in the shade of the sturdy milk cart.

Now, the virulent spirit was like a horde of termites, destroying the carefully crafted timber, eating it up from the inside out.

As the heavy cart cracked and fell, the boy kicked harder at the wood. Even at his vulnerable age of three months, he was not one to be defeated.

His infant legs thrashed, until the milk cart toppled with a low groan, its bow yoke split, the axles shattered, the wheels rolling off in all directions.

Empty milk pitchers clattered across the ground.

As the wood splintered, the spirit fragmented, dissipating into the air, finished.

The commotion caused the villagers to look up from their dance.

The boy's mother hastened to the yard. There, she found her child lying amid the shattered planks. She swept the infant up into her arms and held him tightly.

She chastised herself for her negligence in having handed him off to a maid and not looked in on him even once. So busy had she been celebrating her child that she had forgotten his welfare completely. What might have become of him?

The boy remained unconcerned by the incident. He nuzzled to suckle at her breast. Here was the milk for which he had longed.

His pious mother gazed up into the skies and gave thanks that the boy had survived the accident. Surely, he was divine. She resolved never again to let ceremonial rite become more important than her devotion to the child himself.

Scene III
The Whirlwind

THE KING WAS FURIOUS that his plans to slay the infant had been foiled again. Was there no demon competent to destroy this child? Night after night, he continued to plot. His brow furrowed into a deepening scowl, as he worried over the boy's demise.

One afternoon, the infant lay alone again in the yard, while his mother busied herself about the hearth. She did not mean to neglect her child. He had simply grown too heavy to rest on her hip while she worked. She glanced over her shoulder now and then, watching through the open window as he played.

The boy had recently celebrated his birthday of three months. Comfortable on his belly, he tested his strength, pushing up with his arms to raise his head and chest.

The monkeys in the tree branches overhead leapt with delight at the infant's antics. They chattered and encouraged him, as he reached out for a ripe mango that they tossed his way, the bright fruit rolling in the dust of the yard, the sky a deepening blue above, and the child alight with laughter as his dimpled hands clasped the fragrant gift.

In the house, his mother sang *bhajans* as she busied herself with the usual chores, lighting the fire at the hearth, grinding grain to prepare *capatis*, and churning butter from the cows' fresh milk. She liked to make herself useful, finding deep satisfaction in simple daily duties as sacred offering.

And then, the house went dark, as if the afternoon sun had suddenly been eclipsed, though no such event had been foretold.

Curious, the good woman moved carefully to the window to see what had become of the day. As she peered out into the darkness, the slatted shutters began to rattle.

Immersed in song, she had barely noticed the sound of wind approaching in the distance, but now a storm blustered close at hand, gathering dust as it swirled, howling as if in vengeance.

Indeed, this wind had been conjured up by the king.

With the approaching cyclone, all the land became darker than midnight, for no stars shone in the heavens above. Out in the fields, the cowherds lost sight of their flocks. In the barns, the *gopis* stumbled over their pails. Within the temples, the *pujaris* could see nothing, as they intoned resonant hymns of protection.

The boy's mother groped through the choking darkness, trying desperately to find her child before the cyclone reached the yard.

In the darkening yard, the boy lay without shelter. The monkeys clung to the branches of the trees overhead but could do nothing to protect him. He was at the mercy of the wind, though the wind would show him no mercy, for the king had commanded this wind spirit to do away with the child.

Amid the cloud of darkness that blotted out the village that afternoon, the fierce cyclone indeed lifted the boy as promised and carried him off, in service to the king.

As the wind carried the boy high up into the air, his mother continued to grope about for him in the dust of the darkened yard. Here now was the rough trunk of a tree. Perhaps this was the tree root where she had nestled him. A lone mango rolled away from her hands as she crawled about in search of the child.

She called out to her boy, listening hard for his cry in the rising wind, but the only response came from the monkeys, as they shrieked overhead and shook the branches of the trees. Finally, the good woman hastened to the house for protection. There, she began to wail, as if she herself were a child, or perhaps a mother cow bawling piteously for the loss of her calf.

In the grip of the roaring wind, the child called down to her, but she did not hear him, nor could she have saved him if she had, and so he was carried away into the sky.

The cyclone passed quickly, circling the perimeter of the village, and leaving behind only billowing clouds of dust. Soon, the darkness began to dissipate, and the wind's howl faded away.

Only the grieving mother's cries could be heard.

The neighboring women ran through their yards and down the road. Coughing and holding their veils over their faces, they arrived quickly to comfort the child's mother.

"My boy—" was all that she could say through her tears, but they understood.

Together, the cowherd wives searched for the lost child. They fanned out in all directions. Their colorful skirts blanketed the torn yards and pastures of the village, but the child was nowhere to be found.

He seemed to have vanished into thin air.

Indeed, the demon wind carried the boy higher and higher into the sky. He carried the boy so high up that the air chilled with the altitude and ice crystals formed on his curls.

At the king's decree, the wind planned to blow the boy over to the royal palace. There, he would drop the child from a great height, thus finishing off his brief but divine life, before the child could fulfill the prophecy and slay the unlawful ruler.

The boy, however, was no ordinary infant. Not to be easily overcome, he willed himself to grow heavy as a stone in the wind's clutches.

The rising wind raged at the boy's increasing weight. How could one so tender and small become stoic like a boulder? Soon, however, the wind found himself unable to carry the child any further, struggling even to hover above the village.

The boy willed himself to become heavier yet. He had grown so in the past weeks that his mother had not been able to hold him against her hip while she performed her chores that afternoon. Now, neither would this demon wind hold him.

The wind felt his strength ebbing.

By this time, the boy had grown heavier still, but his great weight was not enough to free him from the clutches of this wind spirit.

And so, the boy reached out and seized the cyclone by the neck.

In the child's hands, the wind howled and writhed, spinning horribly.

The boy continued to hold fast, gazing with fierce determination into the face of the wind.

Finally, the vicious wind fell from the great heights of the sky to the earth below. There, this cyclone was revealed to be the demon it had always been.

The boy landed unharmed atop the dead demon's chest.

His mother rushed to him, with the cowherds and their wives in tow. She lifted the child into her arms and twirled about, so grateful was she that her boy had been released from the raging cyclone.

The cowherds gave thanks that the boy had been found and the wind banished. They knew that he must have protected their village and believed that devotion and charity had blessed them with such a savior as this boy. So, each one vowed to pray more fervently, to give even more generously.

They later resolved at a town hall meeting to plant a greater number of trees than had been uprooted and to dig wells where none had been, in gratitude for the village's deliverance from the cyclone.

Truly, the boy had conquered the whirling wind of the skies and of their minds.

Scene IV
A Handful of Clay

AS THE BOY GREW, he spent more time his older brother. Both were ceremonially named by a traveling *sadhu* whom their father held in high esteem, the boy for his dark complexion and incredible charm.

Although the boy's complexion was dark, his face was radiant with joy. At heart, he was a vibrant prankster, the instigator of village mischief.

He and his brother crawled about in the yard on dimpled hands and knees, their anklet bells jingling, the sound bringing the calves to kick up their heels and the *gopis* to dance.

As they gained confidence, the pair began to explore the land beyond their yard of milk cart and mango tree. They tugged at the calves' tails in a neighbor's field and splashed through the sloggy marsh by the roadside, returning home before dark but covered with mud.

Soon, the boy determined to walk. First, he taught himself to stand by holding fast to the trunk of a flowering tree and pulling himself up, straightening his legs for longer and longer moments amid the humming of the honeybees. With the encouragement of their song, he built strength and balance, until he was able to let go of the tree trunk and stride, like any mature cowherd, through the village.

Ever the mischief-maker, he now unlatched barn doors and gates, releasing the calves at milking time so that they pranced off into the meadows, causing the *gopis* to lift their skirts and chase after the young livestock.

While the *gopis* were chasing their calves, the boy drank from the unattended pails of warm milk and helped himself to handfuls of freshly churned butter in the barns.

The butter he fed liberally to the monkeys, who chattered in the trees overhead.

He made little effort to cover his tracks and became known throughout the village as *navanita chora*, the little butter thief. The *gopis* sang out this epithet among others whenever he wandered by, before making an offering of whatever they had churned that day. Truly, what the boy stole was their hearts.

The *gopis* reported the innocent mischief to his mother, who was more charmed than exasperated by the pranks.

One sultry afternoon, however, one of the boy's companions ran to his mother with a different kind of news. He found her at the hearth, where she was singing *bhajans* as she boiled milk.

"Mother," the child said, "your son—" He stopped to catch his breath, for he had run quickly from the yard to reach her in time.

The boy's mother looked concerned. "What's happened?" she asked, trying to remain calm as her worries mounted. *Had her boy been badly hurt?*

"Your son," the child gasped. "He's eating a handful of dirt."

The boy's mother thought briefly of what the gamboling calves or the milk cart wheels might track across the ground. She dashed out to the yard, where she took hold of her son's muddy hand and scolded him, hoping that he had indeed eaten dirt and not dung or pebbles.

At her vigorous scolding, the boy's full lower lip began to quiver. His wide eyes flooded over with tears, for he could did not wish to upset his beloved *amma*.

His mother softened. "Little fellow," she said, "you steal handfuls of butter from the *gopis*, and they love you all the more for it, but why eat a handful of mud from the yard?"

"I haven't," the child protested. He had not eaten mud but the cosmic matter of all creation, though he knew that his mother could not experience a handful of earth as he did.

He allowed his tears to spill over, expressing sorrow as if he had been betrayed by his faithful companions and now even by his own mother. *Did no one see things as he did? Perhaps in time, they would.*

The other boys looked downcast. Their comrade was a merrymaker, such that most of them had never before seen him cry.

The one who had run to the boy's mother felt sorriest of all, and yet he had not wanted the boy to be sick. He was older and felt protective of him. His chest rose and fell with mature emotion, as he watched the scene between the boy and his mother.

"Did he really eat dirt?" The boy's mother looked up, addressing the entire group of children.

The boys hung their heads at having to relay this unfortunate information, yet they would tell the truth. The boy had indeed eaten dirt.

"I haven't," the boy insisted, raising his head with determination.

The boy's mother shook her head in dismay, her face flushed. *Why did her child persist in denying the truth?*

"If you think that what my friends say is true, then look into my mouth," the boy insisted.

His mother knelt beside him. By this time, she had calmed down and felt sorry for losing her temper. She did not wish to upset her child further, yet she couldn't imagine that his friends were mistaken. She pressed firmly at his chin.

The boy's ruddy lips opened to reveal his truth.

As his mother peered into his mouth, her eyes widened with disbelief. Stunned, she wondered if she were imagining the whole thing, or even dreaming.

Yes, in cavern of her child's mouth appeared to her not mud but the entire glittering cosmos.

Perhaps, this vision might be no more than a trick of the light, the sun's rays glinting off of reflective fragments of stone, she thought. She blinked, as if to clear her sight.

And yet, when she looked again into her child's mouth, she gazed upon all of creation, that which moves and that which does not. Within his mouth appeared the mountains and the sea; the realms of wind and lightning; and the light of the moon and the stars. She beheld the nature of the elements that form the earthly realm, and she beheld heaven, luminous with celestial beings.

Suddenly, she understood the complex nature of mind with its slavish desire for pleasure and futile attraction to possessions, as well as the liberating secrets of time, action, and natural law.

And then, she perceived the entire cowherd village in which they all lived. Here, she witnessed herself kneeling beside the child and peering into his mouth.

At this point, the dumbfounded woman wondered whether she had completely lost her mind.

In this space of not knowing, she realized the foolish vanity by which she had lived, thinking herself grand as wife of the chief cowherd, gratified by their wealth and social position. Her heart bowed to the Lord from which all of creation arises. She felt the ecstatic vibration of her soul, as it merged with the miracle of this myriad existence and the source of all being.

Suddenly, she found herself kneeling on the ground again before her boy, who stood stalwart with his mouth opened.

She touched her child's feet and rubbed the sacred dust over her forehead. She was amazed yet humbled, and regretted having doubted the truth. Yes, what to ordinary village folk seemed a handful of dirt was to her son the entire universe, breathing in all being.

Scene V
The Cord of Love

ONE AFTERNOON, THE BOY sat at his mother's feet, while she churned fresh milk into butter, to be sold at market. The heat of the day made her that much more beautiful, her cheeks gleaming with perspiration, her hair shedding jasmine blossoms across the floor, as she wielded the paddle which stood taller than she.

The boy gazed up at his mother, rhythmic in her work. He was hungry and wanted to suckle.

He climbed up onto a stool and reached out for her. Although he was small, his strength was surprising. His mother found that, with her son holding fast to her arm, she was unable to churn the butter.

She smiled, knowing that the child was hungry. She had tired in the afternoon heat anyhow, so she laid aside the churning rod, seated herself, and lifted the boy to her ample lap.

The boy latched onto her breast, burbling with contentment, as his belly began to fill with warm milk.

His mother crooned to him. She knew no greater joy than holding her child like this. She rocked him gently in time with her breath, as contentment flooded her heart.

A hissing at the hearth interrupted their sunlit reverie, for the pot of milk heating on the fire had begun to boil over.

The good woman sighed. She knew that if she did not remove the pot from the fire, the milk would scald and spill.

She stood reluctantly, pulling the boy from her breast and setting him down gently, before she hastened to the hearth. Certainly, wasting fresh milk was a sin, for so many still went hungry on the distant city streets.

The boy sat at the foot of the churn where she had placed him, unsated. He pounded the earth with his fists, but his mother had turned from him.

He watched as she tended to the milk on the hearth, while he longed desperately to suckle. He reached out for a small stone and flung it at the abandoned butter churn to get her attention.

His strength was greater than he knew, for the clay crock cracked. Whey splashed like a river across the stone floor.

The boy was delighted. If he could not drink of his mother's milk, then he would taste what she had churned, and so he reached into the broken pot for a handful of the pale yellow butter, and sloshed through the whey, out into the yard.

His mother returned from the hearth to find the churning pot cracked and the floor flooded. She noted the trail of small, butter-smeared footprints leading out to the yard and followed them.

She sighed, this time with exasperation.

She spotted her child seated upon an upturned wooden mortar used for husking rice, in the shade of a venerable mango tree. He was feasting on what butter she had churned. Now and again, he fed fingerfuls to the monkeys, all the while glancing furtively about for her, his mother.

The good woman was losing patience in the heat. Already, she had dealt with a mess on the hearth and now she had the cracked butter churn and flooded whey to handle.

She knelt to pick up a small stick from the ground.

Ordinarily, she left discipline to the boy's father, who abandoned any thought of punishment at the sight of the boy's dimpled smile, however irked he had been. Now, his mother determined that their child must learn to curb his pranks.

The switch she chose was small, perhaps a sapling branch recently broken from the trees by the monkeys. It was green and supple and would cause the boy no real harm.

She watched him, speaking to the monkeys and doling out butter, as if he were their king. She could not help adoring him, and yet what a mess he had made, today.

As she walked up quietly behind the boy, several of the monkeys chattered and pointed in warning, like wizened little men in the lower branches of the trees.

The boy turned to catch his mother approaching with sapling branch in hand. She looked as if she meant business, so he jumped down from the mortar and skipped off through the yard, before she could scold him.

He wondered why his mother would chase after him with a tree branch. First, she had denied him her milk, and now she was angry that he had in hunger helped himself to the butter. Her moods made no sense to him.

The monkeys jumped up, miming his mother's scolding, pointing their fingers and clacking their teeth.

Meanwhile, the boy's mother recovered her composure and dropped the ineffectual stick upon the ground. This punishment was not going to work.

She needed a practical solution, so that she could finish the day's chores before her husband returned. The afternoon light was waning, and he might arrive home from herding the cows within the hour. He would be hungry.

The butter had not been churned, nor the *capatis* prepared. The hearth was yet messed with scalded milk, and the kitchen floor flooded with whey. The blessed *sevakas* were nowhere to be found, perhaps fetching water from the river. The house and child had been left in her care, alone.

She centered herself, determining how to proceed. She would set the boy back upon the mortar and tie him to the seat, she decided. The monkeys would surely entertain him, as he would them.

There was no time for further shenanigans that afternoon. She must clean the floor, churn the butter, and prepare dinner, without further interruption.

"You stay there," she told her son, as if he were a little monkey himself, setting him firmly upon the upturned mortar.

She ran quickly to the kitchen cupboard and found a length of string strong enough to hold him in place for the next few minutes. She did not think her child would mind being tied to the mortar.

When she tried to tie the boy to his seat, however, the taut cord fell short by just two inches.

The good woman returned dutifully to the kitchen, fetched another piece of string, and knotted it to the first.

In the yard, she wrapped the new length of string about her boy, but the cord still fell short by the same two inches.

Back and forth she dashed, from the yard to the house to the yard again, until she had tied together every piece of string that she could find in the cupboards, cabinets, and closets, to no avail. The boy continued to wriggle from her grasp, the length of string falling just short of being able to tie him.

From the trees, the monkeys chattered with delight at the child's prowess. They, too, were known for their antics, yet never they could they top the boy in making such glorious mischief.

The *gopis* of the neighboring cottages gathered about the yard. They struggled to hold back their laughter at the boy's antics, as they offered dutiful encouragement to his mother.

Finally, his mother began to laugh, her dress damp with effort, her hair disheveled. No length of string could tie the boy to the mortar.

He was not one to be attached to his seat or to anything else. However delighted her child might be with a piece of fruit that he was given, she had noticed that he would hand off his snack to the monkeys in an instant at the sight of a broad leaf fan, a luminous wishing stone, or an iridescent beetle messenger.

She knew that one day, he might likewise leave the family without a qualm to become a statesman in the city or an ascetic of the mountains. She respected her dignified child, his eyes alight with burgeoning wisdom.

She resolved now to let him roam the yard, as she returned to the house in the hope of completing her chores before sundown. She opened her delicate bangled arms in surrender to him, dropping the knotted string at his feet.

As his mother opened her arms, the child gave up the game. How beautiful she looked, disheveled by her diligent efforts. Suddenly, the mischievous boy wanted nothing more than to please her. He leapt up onto the mortar, where he seated himself with quiet aplomb, in humble invitation. He would acquiesce.

The monkeys gathered at the boy's butter-smeared feet.

His mother glanced back, narrowing her wide eyes in playful suspicion, as she approached her child once more. He looked for all the world like a mature sage, with the simean entourage gathered about him.

Nodding to him in reverence, she began again to wrap the knotted string. This time, the length did not fall short.

What a shame to tie him to this mortar, she thought, though now the boy seemed to welcome her efforts.

The *gopis* gazed on in astonishment from the perimeter of the yard where they had gathered. Truly, this boy could not be bound by any material cord but only by his mother's devotion.

Scene VI
The False Companion

THE DIVINE BOY FLOURISHED, well-fed on the milk of the simple pastoral village. He grew lithe and strong. His hair fell about his broadening shoulders in dark, unruly curls. He adorned his curls with a crown of peacock feathers, wore brilliant yellow silks, and played merry tunes on the wooden flute his father had whittled for him.

His father raised the boy wisely, encouraging his mischievous nature, while instilling in him a sense of responsibility. As the years passed, the elder cowherd entrusted the family's calves to the young lad and to his brother, while he himself continued to care for the mature milk cows.

The boys accepted this new responsibility, pleased that their father held them in such esteem and certain that they were now grown up.

Each day, they carried their flutes and lunch pails out to the pasture. They broke young branches from the trees and brandished them, herding the calves with an enthusiasm known only to youth. They tossed gooseberries and apples back and forth and sang folk tunes. They cavorted on muddy hands and knees, as if they themselves were a part of the herd.

Meanwhile, in the city beyond the river, the ruthless king slammed his fist against the royal desk and tore at his hair, certain that the growing boy would kill him as prophesied. His spies had kept him apprised of the boy's progress, and he now determined to have both the boy and his brother killed while they herded the calves by the river, such that none of the village folk would hear their cries. This time, he would commission a gruesome ogre to do the job.

The chosen ogre was gargantuan and hideously ugly. He was rumored to eat the flesh of stray animals and lost children. Most people ran from him, though the bolder denizens of city spat upon him, jeering and belittling him as their chariots passed him in the streets. So, he learned to hate those who were well-respected—upstanding members of society whom he knew to be vicious hypocrites.

He survived in the shadowy corners of the city, hiding in alleyways to avoid the cruelties of passersby, subsisting on rotting scraps of garbage, the wasted leavings of those who so despised him.

The embittered ogre was particularly irritated by the cheerful games of children. *Why was it that they should be so carefree, while he found not even a moment of joy as an outcast?* Their laughter sent tremors up his spine.

One afternoon, he noticed from a distance the king's ministers processing in their finery. The ogre shrank into the darkness of the alleyway, even as he was revolted by the stench of old bones and rancid milk. Although the local public lived in fear of his brutality, it was he who hid from them.

Had the royal guards finally come to jail, exile, or kill him, due to some histrionic rumor? He could not be held responsible for every lost child. Hordes of beggars and bandits roamed the city streets after dark, while he slept on a ragged blanket behind one of the smaller temples. The priests there showed him no notice but were kind enough not to banish him, either. Once in a while, he found a few *laddus* wrapped in parchment and placed on the ground by the back door.

Now, the ogre waited as the king's ministers continued to march down the street, their boot heels clacking loudly on the cobblestones, their intention to confront him clear.

The men in their finery stopped before him. They tried not to grimace at the ogre's stench and kept a safe distance from his hunched form. Straightening, they announced, "We are here at the king's request."

The ogre tensed and growled, still fearing prison, exile, or death.

And then, the men, with their hair well-oiled and their silks newly sewn, announced the king's decree.

The ogre was taken aback. Indeed, the king had sent these men not to jail, exile, or kill him, but to retain his services, that he might kill two boys of the neighboring countryside. For a moment, he gaped, unable to speak, snuffling through his slobbering jaws.

The king's ministers stiffened. They had drawn straws for this mission, as all had dreaded approaching the ogre. Now, the tallest of the guards placed a hand on his dagger.

The beast, however, recovered from his surprise. "Yes," he growled. "I'll do it." He needed little persuasion, no promise of wealth or power, for finally he was needed by no less than the king himself. He had been given a royal duty to perform. He would have his vengeance on those that had so taunted and plagued him.

The procession of noble ministers sighed, visibly relieved at the ogre's consent, equally confused by his refusal of payment, and eager to return to the safety of the palace.

The ogre was briefed.

He left the city that very night, lumbering along the darkened road to the sleeping village. He harbored no inkling of remorse for the abominable deed he was to perform, for his nature was not even that of an animal.

He slept for a few hours in a ditch by the side of the road.

The following afternoon, he found the lads playing by the river with their herd of calves. He grimaced at their merry-making, quietly observing them from behind a gnarled and barren wood apple tree. Children ran from him, and so he decided to disguise himself as one of their herd.

Chanting a magical spell, he deftly transformed himself into a calf. Then, he loped over to the other calves and began to graze among them. Still, he was larger and uglier than the rest, his eyes like burning coals, his snout distorted, his limbs crooked.

The family calves trotted nervously about, their eyes widening and nostrils flaring at the ogre's approach. Soon, they began to low in distress.

Noticing the herd's odd behavior, the two brothers looked up from their lunch.

The boy harkened to the calves' burbled warnings of lurking danger. He cautioned his brother not to interfere for any reason, left him to keep watch over the flutes and lunch pails, and sauntered over to the animals.

His confidence remained ever undiminished as he rubbed their necks and crooned to them, weaving through the herd until he found the disguised ogre, this false companion.

The *vatsasura's* stench was unbearable, as if he were already dead.

The boy watched the *vatsasura* snuffle and snort, uprooting thorny weeds and nosing about for bruised fruit. He seemed unwilling to taste of the tender green shoots, for he was accustomed to eating rotting garbage.

Nevertheless, the boy sensed the *vatsasura's* power and knew that he needed to act decisively. He waited, steadying himself. Then, he defiantly seized the *vatsasura*, gripping his hind legs with both hands.

The *vatsasura* bellowed wildly, kicking up clods of earth with his front hooves. He was a strong beast, fiercely determined to be of service to the crown. He had found position in society, if he would but destroy this troublesome boy whom the king so feared.

The boy felt himself being hurled about, such that he could barely keep hold of the *vatsasura's* legs.

The family calves lowed and sprang away for safety, gathering about the boy's brother who stood some distance off with the flutes lunch pails.

The boy's brother watched the struggle, his eyes wide, opening his arms to the calves, as they nuzzled against his chest. He feared for the boy's imminent demise, yet he dared not disobey the firm warning not to interfere with assistance of any kind. Although he was the elder of the two, the boy made the decisions for both of them in his calm, self-assured manner.

So, his brother stood with the flutes and lunch pails amid the drove of calves and bowed his head to pray for the boy's safety.

A sharp blow from the *vatsasura's* hooves missed the boy's head and nicked a tree stump, instead.

The boy knew that he must finish the *vatsasura* off quickly to avoid injury to himself and his brother, for he realized now that the *vatsasura* meant to kill them both.

With valiant effort, he took a broad stance upon the earth, gripped the *vatsasura's* legs hard, spun him around, and tossed him up against the high branches of the very wood-apple tree that had hidden the beast, earlier that afternoon.

There, the *vatsasura* lay, slung over a barren bough.

Breathless from the struggle, he glared wildly down at the boy. To kill this youth remained his only chance at gaining the king's favor. He could not bear to return having failed, for then surely he would surely be jailed, exiled, or slain.

Yet, as the *vatsasura* struggled to raise himself, the dry branch supporting him cracked. The heavy beast fell to the ground at the boy's feet.

Now, he lay dead in the grass. His calf-like appearance dissipated as if it had been a dream, and he was revealed to be the bitter and shunned ogre that he truly was.

The boy gazed upon the dead ogre. The gentle lad's brow was untroubled, for he harbored no trace of anger toward the beast. Raising a hand, he quietly blessed the ogre, that his soul might finally be at peace.

His brother stood silent, yet shocked and amazed at the victorious encounter with this interloper of malevolent intent.

Fragrant blossoms from the trees showered the meadow, where the herd of family calves now returned to graze.

The boys agreed not to worry their parents over the frightful encounter that was now resolved. They exhorted each other on the importance of keeping good company and playfully commended each other for their kinship.

Scene VII
The Giant Crane

ONE AFTERNOON, THE TWO BROTHERS herded their calves to the shores of a nearby lake, so that the young animals could quench their thirst after grazing. The calves stood ankle-deep in the lake, lapping at the water, lowing at each other's reflections, snorting fine spray into the air.

Meanwhile, the lads sat cross-legged on the shore. They joked and laughed, conversing through the song of their flutes, and finally took a robust interest their lunch pails.

This day, their mother had provided well for the them. Within the pails they found the curry, rice, fruit, and *capatis* she had packed. The meal was well-spiced and salted. They ate heartily.

When the calves had finished drinking from the lake, the boys knelt at the shore, splashing their faces and sucking in handfuls of the clear, sweet water.

Birds of luminous song and plumage often drank from the lake—peacock, cuckoo, swan, and swallow; those that fed on lotus, mango, raindrops, or moonlight—but the boys were surprised to look up and find an enormous crane in the waters beside them.

The long-necked fisher-bird stood poised. Its beak was long and sharp, like a spear.

Drawing near to the shore, the other cowherd lads began yahooing to each other, staring incredulously at the large bird.

"Look at this fellow," one cried out in amazement. "Who does he think he is, standing so tall and upright?"

The crane peered about unabashed, its eyes darting from one child to another.

One of the youngest boys ducked the crane's gaze and ran for the shelter of a small mango grove.

The boy and his brother, standing in the rippling waters, glanced at each other in confusion.

Their parents had long told them stories of cranes that soared to the heavens and so carried blessings of immortality. Cranes were omens of goodwill. This bird, however, was large and inflated, and seemed to bode nothing benevolent.

The bird lowered his head, gazed intently into the children's bright eyes, and suddenly swallowed the boy whole, as if he had been a fish or a frog.

The boy's brother and the congregation of cowherd lads froze with terror.

The gigantic bird of long neck and spear-like beak began to eye each of the boys, as if deciding who should be next.

The children's blood ran cold. Their knees buckled, as their faces went pale. They were in shock at the sudden loss of their favorite companion. Had he yet been standing on the shore with them, he would have given high-spirited orders to fight or flee the bird, but they were alone, lost without his leadership. They feared for their lives in the gaze of this gigantic bird.

"Run," screamed an older lad, and yet none of them could, held as they were in the bird's panoptic gaze.

Meanwhile, in the crane's throat, the determined boy became like a ball of fire.

The crane gurgled and belched. Swallowing this boy was unbearable. The other cowherd lads now held no interest for him.

Instead, the gargantuan crane lowered his head to gulp the clear waters of the lake through his spear-like beak.

When the lakewaters brought no relief, the bird began to cough up smoke.

By now, the other cowherd lads had recovered from fright enough to make use of their legs and had run to safety. They hid amid a the mango grove to watch the gruesome scene from a distance.

The crane's eyes which had so frightened the children now bulged and watered. No longer able to balance, he wobbled on legs bent back at a sickening angle. The bird writhed, choked, and finally, spat up the boy.

The boy landed on his feet, dripping with mucous as if reborn. Standing knee deep in the lake waters, he threw back his shoulders and gazed fiercely up at this predatory bird, who ate not fish and frogs but children. He must save his companions from the prideful fiend.

The overgrown monster gazed back, the spear-like beak poised to reclaim his prey.

Folding his hands, the boy bowed with reverence.

"No," cried out one of the smaller cowherd lads.

From the mango grove, the other boys gasped. The boy had been returned to them as if by a miracle. *Would he now sacrifice his life?* They had already run to safety. *What could be the purpose of his selfless gesture?*

Some stepped forward bravely to take his place, that he might live. Others longed to be as heroic as he, yet ducked back into the shadows of the trees. All wished that their leader would beat a quick retreat, running to rejoin them, instead of standing stalwart to fight for them.

The bird leaned in, intending to swallow the boy whole again, but the boy was lithe. Leaping up, he grabbed hold of the bird's beak and tore it apart.

One of the smaller cowherd lads turned away, covering his face with his hands. His sweet nature could not endure seeing even a fiend harmed.

The boy persevered in the face of danger. The crane, too overblown to be an omen of benevolence, gave up with a loud cry. His beak torn wide open, he fell down dead in the shallow waters of the lake.

The boy placed a foot gently upon the bird's heart and blessed him that his soul might ascend to its true immortal glory.

The cowherd lads returned to the shore slowly. They remained hesitant at first but soon slapped the boy on the back without reservation. He was ever their revered leader.

They whooped and hollered, splashing water, and then lifted the boy up, carrying him on their shoulders in a victory march back through the fruit-laden trees.

On the way home, the boy and his brother quietly agreed not to tell their parents of this adventure, for none of the cowherd lads had been harmed, and the crane was now dead. They did not wish to be remanded to other duties by their father or to worry their mother.

Still, this tale of the boy's heroic victory over the monstrous crane began to circulate throughout the village, for the cowherd lads were exuberant.

Scene VIII
The Hundred-Hooded Serpent

IN THE COWHERD VILLAGE, the idyllic lakes near the river bloomed with lotus flowers. Amid the flowers, these lakes were inhabited by swans, fabled for their sacred discernment. They cut quiet serpentines through the waters, which reflected the sun overhead as if the lake were a pool of light.

One year, however, during the summer months, an enormous black snake took up residence with his poisonous wives in the largest lake. The waters that they inhabited turned murky and bubbled with toxins. The gentle breeze became entangled with the fumes, carrying them against her will such that the lake shores turned arid.

Nothing grew beside these waters.

The hapless birds that flew overhead fell down dead into the lake, and the snake and his wives fed upon them. The swans disappeared, such that the waters lay forbiddingly dark and still.

The villagers discussed the problem at length. None could determine how to rid the lake of the monstrous serpent that lay coiled in its depths, for anyone who approached the noxious waters fell down dead. They warned their children not to go near the waters, but they did not tell them why, for they did not wish to rouse fear in their innocent hearts.

The children were curious about the newly forbidden lake. One afternoon, several of the bolder cowherd lads wandered further than usual along the riverbanks and came upon the darkened waters.

"Look," said one. "The swans are gone."

The shore was barren and the air dank and heavy, for this lake had become a noxious swamp.

Even so, the day was hot and the boys had wandered far from home, so. several of them felt overcome by an incredible thirst. Forgetting their parents' warnings, they knelt to drink of the noxious lakewaters. There, amid the decaying branches and dead leaves that littered the shore, they themselves fell into a stupor.

Meanwhile, strolling along the riverbank amid the wood apple and star jasmine, the boy and his brother enjoyed the warbling of birds, and yet the day felt strangely still to them, for their companions were nowhere to be found. They had overheard talk of the forbidden lake, as had all of the boys, and were as curious as the next about its waters. Even so, they were not of the mind to disobey their parents.

The boy debated with his brother now, as to whether one or both ought to approach the lake, for he sensed that their missing companions might have gotten themselves into trouble. Finally, he left his brother to herd the calves, while he strode off in search of his friends, calling out their names and whistling to them.

Just as he had suspected, none were to be found in their usual haunts.

Strolling with graceful serenity, he reached the shores of the forbidden lake. There, he saw from a distance that his companions had fallen. Again, he called out to them each by name, but none responded.

The boy approached with quiet discernment to find the fallen lads unconscious by the waters, as were their calves.

He squinted into the depths of the darkened lake. Nothing stirred, but he knew what had happened. No living thing survived on this arid lake shore, and his lifelong friends were in grave danger.

He knelt at their feet in humble prayer. He could not imagine returning that evening, having lost the lot of them. And what of the woe that their deaths would bring to the village?

As he intoned fervent blessings, the cowherd lads began to stir. They coughed and sputtered, gulping in the dank air, as the spark of life enlivened their hearts again.

Slowly, each of the lads revived, though they were yet confused by the poison and the heat of the day.

With immediate danger averted, the boy determined to rid the village of the vile serpent, whom he saw coiled in the depths of the murky waters, like any insidious latent desire.

On the banks of the toxic lake, only one tree had endured, flowering. In years past, a golden-feathered eagle, enemy to all serpents, had roosted in its branches, and so this lone fabled tree stood, resistant to venom, even to the fumes which rose from the lake and choked all other foliage on its shores.

The boy now climbed this tree, fragrant with blossoms on the arid bank where no other living thing had yet been able to survive. From the heights of its fragrant branches, he peered down into the bubbling lake. There, in the depths of the waters, the snake lay coiled, waiting to be roused at the slightest stimulation, by any bird or boy that might sate his endless hunger.

The boy crouched like an agile monkey on a tree branch overhanging the waters.

"Don't jump," shouted one of the younger cowherd lads, but the others silenced him, for they had seen the boy's prowess with the monstrous crane and knew him to be their fearless leader.

The boy inhaled deeply, his dark skin gleaming in the sunlight, his curls loose and free about his broad shoulders as he leapt into the forbidden lake.

The waters were like fire and their stench vile, so the boy wasted no time. He kicked and splashed hard, deliberately rousing the sleeping serpent.

Up from the depths of the lake reared the snake. He glared about to see who dared disturb him.

From the shore, the cowherd lads looked on in horror as the snake raised himself, erect. He was larger than any could have imagined him to be and now, having broken the surface of the waters, he revealed not one but a hundred hooded and venomous heads.

Nonetheless, the boy sported fearlessly, splashing and taunting the thick black snake, its circumference like that of a tree trunk.

The serpent arched his neck, fixed his gaze upon the brash youth, and suddenly struck, his movement faster than the eye could see.

On the banks of the lake, the other cowherd lads cried out for the release of their heroic companion now enrobed in the serpent's indomitable coils. It seemed that he who had just saved all of their lives would now lose his own.

The youngest of the lads turned and ran to the boy's home, to alert his mother of the calamity. She appeared in the doorway smiling, the music of her bangles like wind chimes.

"Mother," he said, breathless. "Your son—"

The good woman remembered that one of her son's companions had once run to warn her when the boy was said to be eating dirt in the yard. "What is it, child?" she asked, awaiting whatever news the boy brought this time.

"The snake," he gasped.

The good woman bewailed her son's plight, crying out to the Lord, the tears of devotion already streaming down her cheeks. Earrings and bangles jangling, she ran through the yard. She was determined to rescue her son from the vicious serpent that so plagued their village.

The other boys' mothers followed after her in a colorful and agitated herd, to the noxious lake.

The boy's mother arrived first, out of breath at the stinking banks. She was prepared to jump into its murky waters and wrestle the serpent herself, but the other women restrained her. It would do the village no good were she to be swallowed by the serpent, as well. The snake was fearsome, and she would not be able to save her boy from the hundred venomous heads.

Still, she struggled on the shore, crying out as the other women held her back.

The serpent did not relent. His menacing eyes glinted like copper in the sunlight.

"No," the boy's mother screamed. The wind ripped the word from her throat, as if tearing out her heart.

The women held her, as the cowherd lads clung to their mothers' skirts, already grieving the loss of their most amiable and graceful companion.

Indeed, the boy, caught up in the serpent's coils, already appeared lifeless.

By this time, the elder cowherds themselves had gathered.

Several of the villagers began to weep. They felt that their lives would be meaningless without this exuberant youth, whose antics brought such joy.

Still, the serpent held the boy fast in his coils. The largest of his hundred hooded heads, tongue flickering like flame, prepared to devour him.

The boy, however, had not been born for such a death. In the grip of the serpent's coils, he appeared to grow in size.

The wicked snake hissed and snorted, but in spite of—or perhaps because of—his venomous malice, he could not maintain his grip on the transcendent cowherd lad. A brief struggle ensued, and the snake released the boy from his coils.

The boy splashed about in a fury and then leapt up onto the largest head, the one that had been about to devour him. Upon the great snake's head, he stomped his blessed feet—distinctively marked with the lotus, goad, thunderbolt, and flag—kicking up his heels, and then he began to dance.

The villagers on the lakeshore stood stunned for a moment, and then they began to dance, singing hymns in praise of the youth's liberation. The women knelt to gather the blossoms that had fallen from the lone surviving tree and tossed them in offering into the lake, as if the waters had been a sacred fire.

The boy jumped from one to another of the hundred serpent heads, their hoods like umbrellas, as the enraged snake reared and struck, missing again and again.

The boy's feet were unrelenting, pounding against the skulls of the snake, bloodying the hoods. His was a dance of dissolution that would rid the village of evil. He danced and whirled to the drumbeat of his own heart, as if in a fervor of ecstasy beyond this world.

Finally, the serpent dropped. His fall made a sick smacking sound against the dark surface of the lake, as the waters heaved and splashed onto the shore with his great weight.

The villagers cheered, even as they ran from the shore to avoid being drenched by the tidal wave of toxic waters.

The boy now prepared to destroy the serpent completely, and certainly would have done so had not the serpent's wives interceded.

Silent until now, they rose from the depths of the waters. In the serpent-realm, their husband was a king, and so the wives were decorated with robes and ornaments.

They brought from their underwater caverns sparkling gems, fragrant oils, and rare flowers, which they now offered to the lad.

The eldest of the wives spoke, her voice hypnotic and soothing. "Please," she said, "let my husband live. He has spared your life, and now you must release him to us, for he is our king."

"How can I?" the boy replied. "His poison would have killed my best friends, and he would have killed me too, had he been able."

"No," the wife said, her voice soft and conciliatory. "My husband is a good king who cares well for us, though he is at times enslaved by his own venomous nature."

The boy knew how cunning serpents could be. Still, he was merciful. Rather than killing the hundred-headed snake, he gave a command.

"Leave, and don't ever come back," he said, meeting the snake's gaze, fiercely.

The hundred-headed serpent, still dazed by the force of the boy's dance, agreed to depart. Grateful that his life had been spared, he swam out to sea with his long and slender wives, never to return.

The waters became clear and sweet again. Soon, the lake mirrored the azure sky, reflecting light as lotus flowers began to bloom. The swans of discernment returned, and the villager's minds were again at peace.

Scene IX
The Forest Fire

DURING THE SUMMER MONTHS, the sun overhead scorched the earth like fire. The shimmering heat was unrelenting, yet the boy and his brother fulfilled their herding duties, eager each day to encounter unforseen adventures of the forest with their companions and the family calves.

They strode along, rarely needing to goad the animals with the green leafy branches which they carried, urging the calves along with their reverberant call and song.

The cowherd lads seemed impervious to the stifling air in their play, dancing in ecstasy with the peacocks, marking each other's foreheads with pollen *tilaks*, and receiving the offerings of trees that bent low to the earth, their branches laden with hot, sweet mango and jackfruit.

The boy playfully dressed his ears with *kadamba* blossoms and praised the trees for providing shade, as well as bounteous gifts of fruit and flower.

Meanwhile, the calves wandered off to graze in a shaded glen. Their hooves crunched through the dry leaves and splintered the twigs that littered the forest floor, as they sought out the stalwart vegetation that yet flourished.

The *kusha* grass they grazed was indeed hardy enough that the villagers wove it into ropes and baskets. The calves ate their fill of this herb, mingling with the goats and wild buffalo that had also sought out the grassy glen. Their hides hot, the calves sidled now and again into the cooling shade of the tangled tree branches.

The sun burned unmitigated, and the forest appeared ethereal, as if it might be an iridescent dreamscape.

The calves rubbed their hides up against the rough tree bark. Their ears pricked up at the sound of the flute, and the boys gently guided them to the sweet waters of a nearby lake.

One sultry afternoon, the bold rays of the sun sparked a parched branch that had fallen to the ground. The dry wood began to smoke and smolder, and soon, a great blaze spread, driven through the brushy undergrowth by the wind's breath.

Unbeknownst to the grazing calves, flame circled the leafy glen, such that when they lifted their heads, they found no possibility of egress. The fire blazed hotter than the sun, shooting off sparks and bringing venerable trees crashing to the ground. The terrified calves began to bellow.

In another part of the forest, beneath the tangle of dark leaves and gnarled branches, the youth and his companions looked up from their sport. Intent as they had been on adorning each other with wildflowers, brilliant in color like fragrant jewels, they had not forgotten their duties.

"The calves," one lad said with a resounding blast of his horn.

Pausing in their revelry, the others glanced about, listening attentively for the sound of pattering hooves or gentle lowing. The only response in the resounding silence was the call of a *kokila*.

The cowherd lads wondered what had kept their animals for so long on this sweltering afternoon.

The boy took up his flute and began to play a simple song, wooing the animals as he did the *gopis*. His curls hung damp with sweat, as his eyes danced across the faces of his companions and off into the trees, where the calves had disappeared.

When the calves did not return, he laid aside his instrument, cupped hands to mouth, and called out to them, his voice resonant.

All expected the animals to trot forth from the trees in lively caravan, but still they did not appear.

This was strange the boy thought, and so he urged the band of cowherd lads to set off in search of the animals. They did so, following the hoofprints and the patterns of *kusha* grass that had been grazed.

Soon, the boys were overcome by smoke. Flames lapped at the forest foliage, turning vibrant leaves and flowers to ash. Trees came crashing to the ground, sending up showers of sparks which ignited the nearby shrubbery. Towers of fire reached up to the skies, and the air was luminous with heat, so that the forest appeared to shimmer and bend.

The cowherd lads were distraught. They feared for the lives of their animals. They had raised these calves since birth. They loved the gentle beasts and knew that their families depended upon the fresh butter and cheese made from their milk.

Suddenly, the boy held up a graceful hand, and the boys halted beneath a banyan tree yet untouched by flame, its graceful branches thick with foliage, its aerial roots strong and arched.

They watched the flames rolling forth from the forest, advancing like fiery tidal waves toward them.

A nearby mango tree began to crack and fall with the heat. One of the younger lads jumped back as a branch, stripped of its long leaves, crashed to the ground.

The rest of the boys stood stock still, as if rooted to the earth, though their minds were leaping and jumping like the very flames that devoured the forest.

Should they abandon the animals to save themselves or risk their lives to rescue the calves? They thought of their mothers and the tears that would be shed were they not to escape this blaze. Then, they remembered their fathers, who would have no livelihood without these cows entrusted to their care this afternoon.

The flames licked at the forest like ravenous tongues, consuming all that they touched.

"We can't outrun the fire," one of the older lads said, with resignation.

The cowherd lads turned to the boy as their leader. They remembered how this boy had saved them from the giant crane and hundred-headed serpent. There was nothing to do now in the face of this indomitable fire but wait for him to speak.

The boy remained calm in the face of the flames that raged like any man's desire.

"Close your eyes," he said. "Don't open them until I tell you to."

One of the younger lads was lost in confusion. He trusted the boy above any other and yet wondered what good closing his eyes to the situation would do. Perhaps they had no recourse. If the fire were certain to take them, they might stand a bit braver with eyes closed. A tear trickled down his cheek at the thought of never seeing his family again.

Another of the younger lads glanced about to see how the other boys would heed this bold order. He would only close his eyes if all the rest did so, too.

Yet another blustered, sure that the animals ought to be saved at any risk to their own lives.

"Close your eyes," the boy said again, his flute in hand, his yellow silk *dhoti* billowing in the heat.

No one disobeyed him. Still coughing from the smoke, the cowherd lads shut their eyes.

The boy looked carefully at each of the cowherd lads, to be certain that none of them yet gazed through lids half-closed. He wanted no tales told of the feat he was about to perform, as had been about the overblown crane and the hundred-headed serpent.

Now, the flames continued to advance toward the boy, who stood strong like one about to step into this sacrificial fire.

He did not.

Instead, he gazed directly into the face of the raging enemy. Then, he opened his mouth and began to swallow the flames, as if he had been a fire-eater at a city festival. The trees of the forest made magnificent torches, standing tall and graceful against the sun. If this day had been night, the sky would have been illuminated by these earthly flames of transformation and renewal.

The cowherd lads stood with eyes closed, their breath coming in short sharp spurts, awaiting their imminent demise.

The boy continued to swallow the flames. Into his mouth they disappeared, flickering in hues of red and gold, blue and green. The blaze was beautiful, an unsurpassed expression of nature's formidable prowess.

Finally, the fire disappeared into his lean belly.

Only then did he call to his companions, who yet stood with their eyes and hands clenched tightly shut. "Alright, you can look now."

One by one, his companions opened their eyes, dreading what they might see—the charred carcasses of their families' calves, the forest like an ash-strewn cremation ground. They were amazed to find instead that the *banyan* tree yet stood above them and that the indomitable fire had abated.

The air was still. Beyond the ravaged glen, trees bore fruit and foliage bloomed. And yet, where were the calves?

Nothing stirred. There was no sound of birdsong, for parrot and cuckoo had long since flown for safety.

The cowherd lads began to call for their animals, their cries resounding through the oddly silent woods. They waited, listening for the sound of hooves against the earth.

"I think I hear something," one said, but then there was silence again.

Their leader lifted the flute to his lips. None could resist the charm of his song, slow and sweet in the ash-strewn forest. In spite of their worries, the boys began to dance. Their feet pattered against the ground, and then there was the sound of hooves in the distance, like a rising drumbeat.

Smoke continued to dissipate, and the calves appeared, lowing and trotting toward the lads, who embraced them, their minds no longer anguished by the raging blaze and now from all longings, liberated.

Scene X
The Mountain Shelter

EACH YEAR, BEFORE THE RAINY SEASON BEGAN, the cowherds' village made traditional ceremonial offerings, to express gratitude for the year's bounty and ensure continued prosperity. The villagers prepared a sumptuous feast of *daal* and milk puddings to feed the poor, while the *pujaris* came down from the hills and performed sacred rites. Gifts were exchanged, the cows well-fed, and the country folk anointed with *vibhuti*, all to welcome the rains, that the grass and crops might thrive.

The cowherds lived in awe of the vast sky and its rains, for the sky might either send forth floods or leave the land in drought, if their sacrifice were not pleasing. Now, preparations for the festival were well under way in hopes that the waters of the sky would bring new life to the earth.

The boy's parents were deeply pious on any ordinary day and even more so during religious festivals. These days, his mother busied herself in the kitchen with fragrant spices, lentils, long-grain rice, fresh milk, and *ghee*. His father prepared to gift the *pujaris* lavishly with cloth and cattle.

The boy and his brother were looking forward to the annual festivities. As they herded the calves through the forest, lush with date-palms and rose-apples, they sauntered along, unconcerned over the imminent *monsoon* season, for the trees provided shelter, their leafy branches spreading like overlapping umbrellas. They spoke of the upcoming festival.

The boy was of an age to question everything. His intelligence was keen, and he did not take folk customs for granted, always wanting to know the reasons behind the rituals. When he and his brother returned home that evening from herding the calves, the boy found his father relaxed, unwinding with the other cowherds at the end of a long and productive day.

At the sight of the graceful lad yet with flute in hand, the father opened his arms, welcoming his son to sit with him.

The boy did so with dignity, though his mind was alive with curiosity at the festive preparations, such that he could not remain silent.

"Why, father?" he asked. "Why do we celebrate the sky and the rain, each year?"

His father was taken aback, but only for a moment. He appreciated his son's curiosity. He turned for a moment from the cowherds, leaving them to exclaim and enjoy steaming cups of *chai* in their revelry, while he spoke quietly with his son.

"We perform these rites to honor the sky and the rains, because our livelihood depends upon them," he explained. "Can you imagine what life would be like if there were a drought, with no crops harvested and no grass for the cows to graze?"

The boy nodded, unconvinced. He knew that he must honor his father, and yet he was not satisfied with this groundless explanation. He wondered whether his father were trying to pacify him or whether he fervently believed himself to be nature's pawn. His luminous brow furrowed.

Seeing that the boy remained skeptical, his father continued. "No matter how hard we work, without the sky's blessing of abundant rain, we would go hungry," he said. "On the other hand, too much rain is no good either, for the land floods."

Then, he seized the opportunity to instill proper reverence in the doubtful boy. "Human effort is of no avail without divine grace," he said, his voice rich in resonance, resounding throughout the room.

The sun was setting. A deep saffron light suffused the space, as the cowherds awaited the evening meal. At their leader's proclamation, they looked about, their eyes wide and kind as those of the cows they herded.

The boy honored his father as progenitor and teacher, and yet this strange turn of faith made no sense to him.

Now, he was torn. He did not believe in such folk myths, and yet how could he possibly defy a father before so many village folk who respected the man as their dignified leader, as well they should. He shook his head in dismay, and then he flushed, his complexion thunderous. Finally, he raised his eyes to meet his father's. He would make his offering to the conversation.

"Father, the Lord can offer no grace to one who does not perform right action, for isn't it true that benevolence cannot be granted to one undeserving?" His gaze was bold, uncompromising.

His father sat silent, astounded. The other cowherds leaned in, listening well to the words of this vibrant youth.

The boy spoke with fervor, urgent to share what he believed. "We each work according to the tendencies developed in prior lives, or even in this one—whether as priests, teachers, warriors, merchants, or cowherds—and the prosperity in our given livelihood depends upon our actions, not on natural phenomena. If we do our work well, being kind to each other here and now, then we need not busy ourselves with outdated rituals."

His father wondered how one so young might hold such depths of understanding. The lad seemed to be gifted with an innate wisdom that far exceeded the insights of even the village elders, who were listening intently to his words.

One day, this young one might travel to the nearby city and become a statesman, his father thought, fondly.

By this time, the boy's brother had come to sit cross-legged by his side.

Seeing that he had commanded the villagers' attention and also the support of his sibling, the boy's voice rose, sonorous and clear as that of the nightingale. "Instead of honoring the sky as a deity for its rains, we might try giving thanks to the cows, who serve us each day unacknowledged, and to the hill upon which they graze. We might well attend to the beggars, who are treated as outcasts."

The villagers began to murmur among themselves. They respected this boy, who at seven years old held himself erect with the bearing of a mature sage. They took his words to heart and began to talk of changing the festival rituals, this year. After all, perhaps he was right. They ought concentrate on giving thanks and doing their work as daily sacrifice, rather than appeasing the deified forces of nature with an annual offering.

Yet, the festival commenced with fanfare at the foot of the *govardhana* hill. Tattered beggars lined up in droves and were fed heaping platefuls of aromatic rice, spiced lentils, chutneys, *samosas*, salted curd, and *puri*, as well as copious platters of milk sweets. Indeed, the mountain appeared to host lakes of *payasam*, in which floated roasted cashews and golden raisins.

The boy himself could not get enough of the *yajna*, calling out, "Give me more," as he stood atop the blessed hill and ate plate after plate full of food. "Give me more," the boy continued to cry, until his brother climbed up to offer a sprig of holy basil, with which the boy was finally satisfied.

The villagers danced and sang, parading around the hill with their cows. They honored the cows for their free-flowing milk, the mountain for supporting the cows, and the *pujaris* for their benevolent ceremonies; however, as the boy had suggested, they did not praise the sky for its rains. These were now regarded as a simple natural phenomenon.

Soon after after the *yajna* concluded, the vast azure sky darkened and began to thunder and crack, splitting with lightning. *Monsoon* season had begun.

The villagers had hoped for rain, but this storm was more than ordinary. The waters poured forth from the sky without ceasing. Wind blew the thatched roofs from the cottages. Hail pelted the soggy meadows. For days, a torrential rain continued to fall, flooding the rivers, fields, and roads, until the villagers feared for their lives.

Remembering the boy's words, the villagers gathered at his family's home, seeking protection. They wondered now about the boy's maverick advice to leave aside honoring the skies this year, and yet they trusted him. The elder cowherds stood quietly, awaiting his guidance.

The boy remained unconcerned. He spoke to no one, as he pushed through the throng and swam out past the swampy pastures, his unruly curls slaked with rain.

He swam with long graceful strokes through the torrid flood, until he reached the *govardhana* hill that stood like a guardian, benevolent with golden stone and fragrant grass, beyond the village.

Now, its grasses were sodden. Mud slid from the mountain, uprooting saplings and sacred herbs, and tossing boulders that splashed and sank in the rushing floodwaters.

The boy knelt and reached his hands out to the foot of the mountain. He strained, but nothing happened. Concentrating intently, he tried again, to no avail. Finally, whispering a few words of prayer, he focused, and the mountain began to move.

With the assurance known only to youth, the boy raised the hill upon one finger, for at his age, he knew nothing to be impossible. He had become one with his *giriraja*. Then, he blew upon a horn, summoning his parents to bring the villagers and the cows, that they might take refuge with him.

A great crowd of country folk swam through the flood, amid the floating milk pitchers and butter pots. Colorful cotton clothing ballooned, as the villagers tried to save their children and animals.

The waters continued to rise.

One woman lost the hand of her child, who began to float off through the waters. She cried out, and a village elder, struggling to herd his own family through the flood, reached out and grasped the child's shirt, just as the little one would have been lost.

None knew how they would survive, yet they heeded the youth's call and struggled to reach him.

In the distance, the boy held the *govardhana* hill up effortlessly with one finger, as if he were an elephant offering a lotus flower with its trunk. His complexion was radiant amid the storm clouds.

The villagers crowded into the shelter, taking refuge beneath the *giriraja* that the boy supported. Truly, he was their refuge.

Rain continued to fall. The villagers could hardly hear each other speak over the din of rushing water and crashing thunder. They huddled together, holding onto one another.

For seven days, the boy stood steadfastly without food or drink, holding up the *govardhana* mountain.

After seven days, the furious sky relented, surrendering to the youth's devout strength.

Indeed, the thundering clouds passed. The winds quieted, and the rain subsided. The sky opened, once again clear and azure, illuminated by the sun.

As the water levels drained, the villagers stepped out from beneath the hill into the light. The boy gently replaced the *giriraja* on its earthy foundation.

Seeing that all was now well with their land, the villagers began to sing and dance. Yes, the sky was divine, as were the cows, the meadows, the river, the forest, the mountain, and certainly this luminous boy, though performing ritual now seemed less important than expressing gratitude through devout daily duty.

One day, the boy would sing of devotion and duty on the distant battlefield of Kurukshetra, such that people throughout the land would be awaken to a new way of living.

Now, the luminous youth returned home with his family to tend the calves.

SUDDENLY, ONE OF THE GOPIS who had remained quietly behind the scenes called out to the rest of them, yet immersed in the play.

"Look, here. I've found his footprints."

A curtain of silence came down upon the childhood drama, and the flower-strewn stage was abandoned.

The *gopis* gathered to examine these newly discovered footprints along the path. Indeed, the soft footfalls matched the graceful size and shape of the boy's feet, imprinted with the lotus, goad, thunderbolt, and flag.

Now, the *gopis* turned with delight to follow in their *gopala's* footsteps, through the darkened forest.

IV

PRIDE

THE GOPIS STROLLED ON along the path, lit only by the ruddy moon, in eager anticipation of reunion with the boy. Here and there, his footsteps seemed to dance, through the fallen twigs and burgeoning moss, across the long mango leaves and fragrant jasmine blossoms.

Suddenly, their faces fell, for they had come upon another smaller set of footprints intertwined with his.

They wondered who she could be and glanced from face to face to see which one of them was missing. They imagined the boy's graceful arm slung about this favored milkmaid's shoulders and the lilting songs he would sing to her. What joy would flood her heart at his sidelong glance.

"But why would our beloved boy choose to be alone with her when he could be adored by all of us?" said one. She voiced what each was thinking.

Each girl longed for nothing more than to sit by the river with the boy, to watch the cows graze under his protection, to listen as he improvised melodies on his flute, to dance with him amid the overgrown wildflowers; yet none sought to be singled out as different from the others.

The surge of excitement brought on by the first glimpse of his definitive footprints was now quelled at the sight of his companion's.

"She's a thief," one of the *gopis* cried out suddenly, for the traitor among them had stolen away with the one boy who was a favorite companion to all.

The village maids flushed with agitation as they now followed both sets of footprints, his strong and self-assured intertwined with the delicate steps of the favored *gopi*.

Time spent with this cowherd lad meant more to the *gopis* than keeping house and caring for their families. The tenderness they felt for him was different from that which they felt for their husbands and children. They knew that they were needed by their families, and yet in spite of the expected commitments at the hearth fire, they rushed from their cottages to revel at the river with this boy whenever they could—waiting breathlessly for their children to nap, leaving aside the butter half-churned, and romping out into the forest before their husbands returned, their faces fresh and bright like the flowers along the path.

"What more could he want than such devotion? What does this particular girl have to offer that we do not?" said one.

Their desperate ruminations were interrupted by the sudden disappearance of one set of footprints—hers. Yes, those that continued along the tangled forest path were surely the boy's, recognizable by their signature grace and markings, though his footfalls had deepened, as if he had lifted and carried his slender companion, whose feet may have been bruised by tufts of dry grass. And then appeared the marks of the balls of his feet.

The *gopis* gasped at the half-prints, where the lithe boy must have stood on tip-toe, stretching up to pick flowers from the arched bowers of a tree for her.

They drove themselves to distraction, imagining that the two had sat alone together while he braided the blossoms through her long tresses, that the two had gazed delightedly into each other's eyes as he wove for her a fragrant crown.

The saving grace was their assurance that nothing more than wildflowers could have passed between the two, for the innocent boy was contented with his simple life, fulfilled on the sap of his effervescent inner joy.

This was why the *gopis* felt carefree when they were with him, as if they too had been liberated from any worldly worries or responsibilities. The boy wanted nothing from anyone, accepting each as she was in the everlasting moment, and so they overflowed with bliss in his presence.

Now, they grieved at having been abandoned by their beloved *gopala* for reasons they could not understand. What did the chosen milkmaid have over them?

And then, the herd of them came upon her, alone and despairing.

"Why is he no longer with you?" several of the girls demanded at once. They were in a fury over having been abandoned, confused by the tears of this favored maid, and yet overwhelmed by curiosity as to what had passed between them.

The abandoned girl did not balk but answered on cue, grateful to have been found by her companions.

"I must have peeved him with my demands," she said, her tears flowing like the moonlit river.

"As we wandered deeper into the forest, pride filled my heart.

"'Surely, I must be the favorite companion to this boy with whom the other *gopis* long to frolic,' I thought. 'Yes, I am indeed special, more devout than the rest.'

"It seemed so, for as we walked, he reached up into the highest branches of a tree to pick flowers in full bloom for my hair. Then, his gentle hands wove a sweet garland, for me alone.

"The fragrance of jasmine was intoxicating, and as we continued to stroll, I began to wonder how much prowess I held over his heart. Even as we were laughing and enjoying the moonlit fruit and flowers, I determined to test his feelings for me.

"'I'm tired,' I said. 'I can't walk any further.' Then, imagining myself to be his cherished princess, I told him with a glance meant to be coquettish, that he might carry me wherever he liked.

"Of course, he acquiesced. He is ever debonair in his youth, dignified as befits one of royal birth. He got down on one knee before me, as if to lift and carry me.

"Gazing upon him, I thought not of my love for him but of how I surpassed all of you, with the charm of my smile and the sweetness of my song. I was certain that my attentions to him must have been more pleasing than any of yours, and that now I was his one and only, that he was indeed mine.

"My bosom swelled. I imagined that he might carry me to a moonlit clearing in the forest, where we would feast on fig and mango, amid star-eyed jasmine that would perfume the night for us alone.

"Only then did I realize that he had disappeared.

She stopped and sobbed, as she then described her tears of that moment.

"My tears watered the mimosa blossoms that grew wild along the path.

"'Where have you gone?' I called out into the darkness. 'Are you not still my most cherished *gopala*? Pious boy of tender strength, tell me where you have gone, for I can do nothing now but weep for you.'

"Needless to say, he did not reappear—though now all of you have."

The newly arrived *gopis* listened, their eyes wide like those of the deer. They were astonished that this gallant boy who meant everything to them would abandon them so cruelly, after they had left home and hearth for him this night.

Together, they roamed the dark forest, exploring every glade and grove. As they searched the depths of the woods, they reached a point at which they no longer wished to continue. The bleak night was impenetrable.

They could wander no further. Neither could they return home, for they were truly lost.

Mired in despair, the *gopis* became convinced that they would not again know joy, until their beloved companion returned to them. They longed only for his light-hearted dance, his carefree smile, and his simple melodies.

They began to sing of their longing for his return and of how they loved him, that he might hear one sweet word that pleased him and reappear.

As the *gopis'* tears gave way to song, jasmine bloomed ardently, like stars amid the dark night.

V

The Heart Song

Victory to your birth that blessed this land.
Good fortune reigns here, now.
The cowherds rejoice in abundance,
but we weep, searching the forests for you.
Have mercy, and show yourself.

Your eyes are lotus flowers
that bloom in spring waters.
The heart surrenders to your glance.
We are your simple servants, now.
This longing for you feels like dying.
Show yourself.

From the serpent, from the rain,
you saved us. From wind, fire,
and wicked disaster, you saved us.
Why let us die now?

You are not a cowherd's son. You
are the soul, the breath of creation,
born as a village lad to protect us.
You rose like the dawn
in answer to our prayers.
Do not leave us in despair.

Flawless jewel of these hills,
you are the good fortune of our village.
Whoever kneels at your feet
is released from the torment
of desire, of dying. Rest
your lotus petal palms upon
our heads, for we surrender.

Your courage conquers misery.
Pride bows to your smile.
Accept us however you like—
as friends, as servants.
Show us your face in bloom
like the lotus, that we may kneel
at your feet.

Your feet follow the hoofprints
of the grazing cows. Your feet
dance upon the serpent's head.
Adored by good fortune, your feet
crush the sins of simple folk like us.
Stand firmly upon our hearts
that we may be free of sorrow.

Your voice is tender, your words endearing.
The renounced and learned fall at your feet
and sacrifice, but we simple *gopis*
are fainting fools. You are our hero.
Revive us with the nectar of your song.

Stories of your immortal feats
save the afflicted. Hearing these stories told
sanctifies the sinner and sustains the saint.
Sages and poets praise you for all to hear;
theirs is true generosity.

We meditate upon your glance,
your laughter, and your stride.
Time and again, you have stolen
away with us to touch the heart.
We would forget you, but we cannot.
Show yourself.

As you wander with the grazing calves,
your feet, tender as lotus petals,
may be bruised by stones or thorns.
So, we agonize. Show yourself.

When you return at dusk,
your dark curls wild,
your face smudged with blue dust
kicked up by the calves,
we rejoice. Show yourself.

You sanctify all who surrender
at your feet, your feet
like lotus blossoms,
like jewels upon the earth.
Beloved boy, you are our comfort
and our peace. Soothe our troubled
minds. Show yourself.

Your lips kiss the flute and fill it
with tremulous song, your song
the immortal nectar that heals
lust's wounds. Let us be your flute.
End the despair of this separation.

By day, you disappear into the forest;
a moment spent without gazing upon you
feels like eons to us. When you return
at dusk, curls tangled about your face,
we drink in your gaze. How cruel then
seems the blinking of our eyes.

We've left our husbands and sons,
renounced our families for the music
of your flute; but now you've abandoned us—
for what? Show yourself.

We long for your presence.
Our hearts rise with anticipation
of your laugh, your sidelong glance.
We would lay our heads upon your chest.
We have certainly lost our minds.
Show yourself.

A glimpse of you relieves the sorrows
of all who dwell in this village—
cowherds, swans, maidens, monkeys,
peacocks, and calves—and blesses all
of creation. Without you, we are
heartsick. Give us the medicine we need.
Show yourself.

Now, your tender feet may be bruised
by stone and thorn. We would hold them
gently, and rest them upon our hearts.
We live only for you.

VI

Renewal

THE LAST NOTES OF THE SONG wafted into silence on
the fragrant breeze, and the *gopis* looked up to find the
boy before them. His golden silk *dhoti* shimmered in
the moonlight, and a fresh garland of forest flowers
hung fragrant around his neck. He was ever beautiful
to them.

The *gopis* rose as if from a swoon, their eyes
wide, their faces tear-streaked, their breasts heaving.
One clasped his right hand in hers. Another wrapped
his left arm, fragrant with sandalwood, about her
shoulders. Yet another cupped her hands beneath his
mouth, that he might relieve himself of the *betel* nut
he chewed.

A solitary girl bit her lower lip in anger at his
disappearance and glared about from beneath knit
brows, trying to restrain her tears. Another stood
with eyes closed in ecstasy, imagining that the boy
had returned only to her. Yet another drank in his
glance as if it were lotus nectar, her eyes wide and
unblinking, insatiable. Still another drew him into
her heart, where she embraced him. Blissful as
any ascetic, she overflowed with ecstasy, her limbs
rippling like the river.

Sorrows were soon assuaged.

The boy wanted nothing more than to fulfill the
devotional longings of these village *gopis*, as if at his
tender age he were a venerable sage. He stood among

them, radiant. Then, he led the *gopis* back to the banks of the river, fragrant with jasmine and crown blossoms that hummed with the bees drunk on their nectar.

There, the river's rippling hands heaped sand upon the banks that he might sit, and the moon played gracious hostess, illuminating the waters. The clarity of the moon's light promised the blossoming of spring, though these were yet autumn months.

Gathered with him by the river, the *gopis'* minds cleared. The persistent ache of longing was now relieved. They arranged their shawls, red with *kumkum*, upon the sand as a cushion for the boy.

"Sit here," they urged, and at their sincere invitation, he sat upon the shawls that had been folded and piled for him, though his true seat was in the heart of each girl.

For the *gopis*, he was the luminous truth that pervaded yet transcended their rustic lives. This love for him made each one vibrant, as if lit from within. No one like this boy had been seen before by any of them, not even in their dreams.

Now, the *gopis* gazed at him with their eyebrows arched coyly, their glances sidelong, and their smiles playful. They stretched his lithe limbs into their laps and stroked his hands and feet.

They adored him, though they remained frustrated by his prolonged absence that night. They could not understand why he had abandoned them, and so they questioned the boy about his absence, and then they dared asked him about love.

"Some love only as they are loved in return," said one girl.

"Others love even those who don't love them," said another.

"Still others live loving neither those who love them nor those who don't," said a third.

Soon, they all chimed in. "Of these three, whose love is true?"

The boy sat radiant in the moonlight, as he began to speak. "Fair-weather friends who love only for the love they may gain in return are not true friends," he said, with a careless shrug.

Then, he paused, gazing into the rapt eyes of each *gopi*. He praised them all for the beauty of their faces and even moreso for the beauty of their hearts. Only then did he continue with the teaching, his voice clear amid the intoxicating fragrance of jasmine blossoms.

"Those who love selflessly, without desire for what they may gain in return, love in two ways. Their love is like that of either a parent or a teacher. And who could fault them?"

The *gopis* listened intently to his every word.

Now, the boy determined to reveal the luminous truth to them. "Those who love no one, however, may be of three kinds."

The *gopis* nodded, waiting breathlessly for him to continue.

"It's possible that those who love none are fulfilled by the inner light of the soul, that they've awakened to be one with the soul of all being.

"On the other hand, such people might be uncouth—feeling no gratitude or respect for anyone."

The girls gasped in sudden despair. Could it be that their beloved *gopala* had disappeared into the night because he found their love unworthy or cared nothing for them?

"Rest assured," the boy said, noting their distress. "I am like none of these three. I left you not because I did not love you. I hid myself for your sake, so that your devotion might increase." He paused, a vulnerable youth considering his words carefully. "I disappeared to awaken true love."

The *gopis* looked on, incredulous.

The boy hurried to explain himself. "Consider one impoverished who works hard to earn a moderate sum and then loses it. The poor man can think of nothing but what has been lost.

"Like this, when I disappeared, you could think of nothing but me. Already, you've given up concern for wealth and social standing. You've set aside the tenets of scripture, with their ritual promises of a better life hereafter. Tonight, you've even abandoned the hearthfire for my sake."

One by one, each girl began to smile.

"Yes," the boy said, pleased that the light of understanding was dawning upon them. "I disappeared tonight to rouse your longings, to enliven your praises, to inspire even greater deeds of devotion. Yet," he consoled them, "I continued to watch over you all the while.

"And what a song you have sung. Were I to strive for countless eons, I could not equal such devotion and surrender, this outpouring of love tainted by no worldly desire whatsoever."

The *gopis* began to sigh with pleasure, but the boy did not mean to flatter them. He continued, his voice growing rhythmic and strong, with an even deeper revelation. "You love my soul more than you do your own flesh-and-blood kin. You've broken free from the bondage of worldly life.

"As a cowherd lad, I am nothing in the face of such love." He paused again, that they might take in the full force of his climactic instruction.

"Now, let the overflowing devotion of your own hearts bring you everlasting bliss."

VII
The Dance

THE GOPIS RECEIVED the boy's words with reverence, for this simple cowherd lad embodied the timeless wisdom of scripture. Their every doubt was assuaged.

Now, the boy wanted to dance with them. Was this not the reason he had called them to the river in the first place on such a fragrant autumn night? He leapt to his feet and bowed in courteous invitation.

The *gopis* joined hands to form a circle without beginning or end, and began to step with delicate rhythms across the earth. Each girl felt as if the boy danced only with her, for now each had truly surrendered her heart to him.

Shooting stars appeared like fireworks in the sky, as if the celestials had gathered in their starlit chariots to bless this celebration. The sky thundered with the sound of kettledrums. Flower petals showered upon the riverbanks.

The *gopis'* anklets, belts, bangles, and bells jangled, as did those of the boy, all of their feet dancing across the earth to the music of the spheres.

The boy shone like an emerald amid the golden bangle of *gopis*, their smiles contented, their eyes wide with delight.

The circle bent and swayed as the *gopis* danced, their waists supple and their dresses damp with perspiration. Their earrings dangled and swung against their cheeks. Their faces were bright, like bursts of lightning amid storm clouds, as they sang the glories of their *gopala*.

One cried out in harmony with the boy, improvising upon his melodies, her song an octave higher than his.

He was delighted and said so, at which point she livened up the tempo, causing him to cheer even more.

One, exhausted with braids and bracelets flying loose, clung to his neck.

One kissed his hands, smeared with sandalwood paste and fragrant as lotus blossoms.

One, her face lit by the reflected light of her earrings, pressed her cheek to his.

One playfully received the *betel* quid from his mouth into hers.

One, dancing to the sound of her anklet bells, became tired and pressed his palms to her heart.

Each played at being wedded to him, in her innocent elation.

Truly, the village *gopis* danced with the Lord that night, their faces shining like full-blown lotus blossoms, jasmine petals falling from their hair.

The buzzing bees became an orchestra that stepped up the dance, as did the tinkling of the *gopis'* anklets, belts, bangles, and bells.

The boy delighted in the *gopis* as any child might his image in a mirror—hugging and kissing, pressing palm to palm, tossing playful glances about, all the while smiling—he their youthful *gopala*.

By this time, the *gopis* had lost their ornaments and flowers to the earth beneath their feet and their dresses had slipped from their shoulders, but they held not a care in the world. All that mattered to them was this blissful dance with the Lord.

The moon shone radiant and still amid the stars, that this night might never end.

Whosoever hears told or tells of this dance,
whosoever celebrates life as a dance
with the Lord who lives in the heart,
has all desires fulfilled and is liberated.

Epilogue

Just east of the river where the boy and the *gopis* reveled, the unlawful king still feared for his life. Sorcery had failed to destroy the boy, so this time, the king sent not for gypsy, demon, or ogre, but for a trusted minister. He commanded the minister to visit the nearby pastoral village and bring both the boy and his brother back to the palace.

"Such is my wish," he decreed.

The minister knew better than to contradict the royal ordinance, however, unlike this cruel king, the minister was wise and fair-minded.

"Maharaj, please remember the prophecy," he said, bowing in deference.

"Do you think I have forgotten it?" the king blustered. "Why else would I ask you to bring the boy here? Because of the prophecy, we must do away with him—once and for all, here and now."

"Yes, Maharaj," the minister answered. "I, too, was thinking of the prophecy, which foretold that the boy would slay you, rather than the other way around."

The king glared at his minister, who bowed even more humbly and continued.

"Your resolve is noble, but were we to bring the boy into your palace, no one can say for certain who would slay whom," the minister explained. "Would it not be wise to leave him as he is, contented with the cows in the forest?"

"You must bring him here," the king shouted. His face flushed with passion beneath the golden crown, which now glinted, garish and askew.

And so, the minister acquiesced, departing the next day in one of the royal chariots.

Although the minister had long been loyal to the king, his heart soared with delight at the thought of meeting the divine child, of gazing into his luminous eyes, wide like full-blown lotus blossoms, vast as the infinite sky.

As the chariot left the city behind and began to jounce along the rural road to the cowherds' village, the minister considered his life in politics. He had sacrificed his every virtue in service to a wicked and unlawful king, for the sake of wealth and power. How unworthy he felt now of the boy's grace, and yet his sins must have been forgiven, for he was indeed to meet one whose holy feet, adorned with *kumkum*, dispelled all sorrows.

A small herd of deer leapt across the road, and the minister broke from his reverie to admire them, noting their appearance as an omen of blessing for the journey.

He looked forward to arriving in the simple village, to that moment when he would jump down from the chariot to prostrate at the shining feet of the boy, and also at those of his brother and the band of cowherd lads.

Perhaps the boy would lay hands on his bowed head in blessing, the boy's palms fragrant like that mythical flower of a hundred scents, his smile like spring mist after a cold, dry winter.

Already, the minister considered the boy to be his dearest friend, and even his kin.

The royal chariot arrived in the cowherds' village, just as the sun was setting. In the red glow of late afternoon, the minister yet found the boy's footprints easily, for they were distinctively marked with the lotus, goad, thunderbolt, and flag. As he gazed at the foretold markings, his eyes overflowed with tears of devotion. How blessed was he after giving his life over to vile political intrigue now to find the boy's footsteps along the path.

He descended from his high seat, prostrated upon the earth, and rubbed the dust, made holy by the touch of the boy's feet, upon his forehead. Already, he was inebriated with bliss, though he had not yet encountered the boy himself.

Following the boy's blessed steps along the path, the minister soon found the boy and his brother milking the cows in their yard. They were child-like yet powerful, of fair complexion with unruly curls and dancing eyes.

Again, the minister's eyes overflowed with tears of devotion. He fell to the ground, this time at their feet.

The boys laid their hands upon the minister's head in blessing and then embraced him.

"Welcome," they said, as if they had been awaiting his arrival all day.

"Thank you," the minister replied with grave humility.

He was so overcome by their fond greeting that he nearly forgot his purpose in seeking them. Now, he remembered the king's mandate, and his throat constricted, yet he prepared himself to make the invitation as the king had commanded.

Coughing in introduction, he spoke on official business. "I am here as a representative of the king."

The boys listened with rapt attention.

The minister hesitated. How could he possibly invite two such trusting young lads to their death? Yet, he knew that he must indeed return to the king, and that outcome of this journey would necessarily be his head or theirs. Setting his jaw with determination, he disregarded the pricking of his conscience and continued in his service to the king.

He spoke with majestic resonance. "The king would like to invite you to a royal wrestling match. He requests your presence, immediately."

There, he had done it. Although he had neither wife nor children of his own, he found himself feeling fatherly toward the boys, as if he wanted only to protect them. He stroked his greying beard, half-hoping that these boys would muster the spunk to refuse his invitation outright or at least to politely decline, romping off into the sunlit meadows of the village, where they would never be seen or heard from again. Ah, if only the king would forget about the boy and the prophecy. This was but a child with a luminous future ahead of him.

The boy noted the minister's chagrin. He knew well of the king's ill intentions but resolved to face this latest challenge. "We accept," he replied, without hesitation.

Then, the two brothers began to cavort, making a play of showing their lithe and youthful muscles.

The minister nodded, sighing with resignation. He had succeeded in his mission for the king as no one else had, and yet what of his soul?

Nonetheless, the party departed from the village the next day at sunrise. The boys bore gifts of their family's finest milk, butter, and cheese for the king. They regaled each other along the way, as the minister's golden chariot carried them along the unpaved country road toward the royal city.

The king's city stood behind crystal gates. Ornamented with gold, they arced up into the sunlight. The chariot passed through, majestically.

Behind the gates stood granaries built of gleaming copper, gardens planted with fragrant and exotic flowers, and colorful mansions inlaid with gold and precious gems. Everywhere were hung flower garlands, silk scarves, festoons, banners, and twinkling lights. Plantain trees grew heavy with fruit, and palm trees fanned out, laden with coconuts. Peacocks enjoyed free roam of the lawns.

The boys decided to camp in a public garden for the night. There, they feasted upon a simple repast of rice, lentils, and *payasam*.

They remained unconcerned about the outcome of the impending wrestling match, and they slept deeply.

Having fulfilled his duties, the minister departed bearing their gifts for the king, who would summon the boys to the royal stadium the following day.

That night, the king found sleep elusive. He tossed and turned on his embroidered sheets, yet troubled by vivid nightmares. He dreamt of finding himself alone and unclothed; he dreamt of being poisoned;

and finally he dreamt of death's cold embrace. When the sun rose, casting golden light across the streets already bustling with vendors, he was exhausted.

Bleary-eyed as he was, he dressed carefully, allowing himself to be decorated with finely woven cloth, golden ornaments, and flower garlands, in honor of the wrestling match planned for this day upon which he had determined to rid himself of the child nemesis. He appeared strong and resplendent, though his eyes were deeply shadowed from lack of sleep and worry.

A tumultuous crowd gathered in the arena to watch the wrestling match, billed by the palace as the event of the season. They had traveled from all corners of the city and even from the surrounding countryside, not for fascination with bloodsport but because they longed to be blessed by the divine *gopala*.

Waiting in the stands, they recounted the boy's miraculous feats. Excitement rose as they spoke of how he had banished the monstrous serpent, swallowed the raging forest fire, and lifted the mountain with one finger.

Trumpets blared, announcing the commencement of the match.

The boy and his brother emerged, glorious. They were small but stood with confidence, as comfortable in this crowded royal arena as they were with their calves in the forest.

The crowd's shouts rose as the king's master wrestler approached the boys.

"Those who please the king prosper," he roared. "Those who disobey come to a bad end." He stood like a mountain. "The king has requested that we engage in a public wrestling match. You boys should do as you are told."

The boy knew that the king had planned this wrestling match as yet another attempt to end his life, and that of his brother, as well. Still, he stood up to the behemoth wrestler.

"We have every intention of pleasing the king," he replied with elegant deference, "but we are young and have lived all our lives in a small rural village. We've only wrestled in play, while the calves grazed."

The royal wrestler glared at the boys, anticipating a refusal to fight. The king would be furious if the match did not go off well, now that the entire city had gathered in the stands.

The boy knew what the wrestler was thinking and addressed his concern, directly. "This crowd expects a fair fight." he said. "How much more righteous would the match be if you faced qualified contestants, rather than boys like us."

The king's wrestler grew red in the face. "You are undoubtedly strong, for your feats are well-known. The king will not take no for answer." His stern roar put an end to the discussion.

Huge and lumbering, he himself faced off with the boy, while another strongman entered the arena to combat his brother.

The children took their stances, and the match began without further delay.

The boys and the wrestlers intertwined arms and legs, grunting with the effort. They engaged fist to fist, elbow to elbow, chest to chest, and head to head. They rolled about, now catching a stranglehold and again lifting and throwing each other to the ground, as each sought victory.

The king looked on, watching over all.

In the stands, the women began to murmur, fretting that the match was unfair, as the boy had predicted that they would.

"These lads are of tender limb," they said. "Surely, we are committing sin in watching their demise. The law tells us not to bear witness to wrongdoing such as this."

Others spoke out loudly against the match. "The wise would not lay eyes upon such an indiscriminate contest."

Still more folk, lost in the bliss of the boy's presence, spoke of his village comrades. "How blessed are the cowherd lads each day to behold this boy's playful smile and hear the melodious notes of his flute," they said.

In the arena, the boy's face broke out in a sweat, like a lotus blossom beaded with water droplets.

Meanwhile, his brother's cheeks flushed with the heat of the match. His eyes glowed.

As the boy continued to struggle with the king's wrestler, he listened attentively to all that the crowd said of him. His heart was roused with compassion. He understood that the women in the stands feared for his life, as they would for that of their own sons. In his sympathy for them, he resolved to finish the match quickly, that it might no longer trouble such gentle onlookers.

His hands were like thunderbolts, as he pummeled his opponent.

The king's master wrestler fought on, sore and exhausted. His joints ached. He punched at the boy's chest with both fists.

These blows felt to the boy as might flower petals to an elephant.

With fierce determination, he gripped the wrestler's fists—swinging him around, around, and around, and finally releasing him to slam down against the earth.

The onlookers rose in the stands and cheered. The king's finest wrestler had fallen like an idol, defeated by this cowherd lad.

The boy's brother had already beaten his respective opponent, who lay on the ground, as if he were a tree uprooted by wind.

The king gaped down at the scene. He had not imagined that the match would finish so quickly, nor that his greatest wrestlers could be defeated by anyone, particularly not such young boys who had no training in the finer points of footwork, back arch, takedowns, and pummeling.

Dumbfounded, he raised a royal hand, motioning for other wrestlers to enter the arena, but the boy and his brother defeated them all, easily.

The remaining strongmen disbanded in fear.

In the center of the stadium, the boy and his brother began to dance. The bells of their anklets rang out with joy, as they kicked up their heels and stomped their feet. The other cowherd lads rushed into the arena to join them, blowing upon their horns, exultant in victory.

From the stands, women rejoiced and holy men pronounced blessings.

Only the unlawful king glowered and grimaced.

With a furious sweep of his arm, he silenced the jubilant crowd. Then, he spoke that all might hear. In a deafening voice, he ordered the boys expelled from his kingdom and their pastoral village pillaged.

"Blind their father," he cried out, "and murder mine, for he has taken their side." He raged, completely incoherent in his orders, waving his sword high in the air, the glittering crown askew and slipping from his head.

Suddenly, the boy bounded from the arena up into the stands. He grasped the unlawful king by the hair, as an eagle might a snake. Then, he tossed the wicked man down from the heights of his throne into the arena.

The crowd gasped in amazement. They wondered whether the boy and the king would now engage in hand to hand combat, but there was no time to consider this possibility. The king landed with a heavy thud in the stadium, where he was immediately pronounced dead.

The boy leapt from the jeweled throne back down to the stadium, where he began to stride about, dragging the king's inert body back and forth for all to see. Child that he was, he stood like a mighty hero with a slain lion.

So, the wedding prophecy of the king's death was fulfilled. The vast sky sounded with the thunder of kettle-drums, and fragrant blossoms showered upon the earth.

But the celebration was not complete. In the stands, several ladies of the court bemoaned the king's death. He had been kind to them, bestowing upon them every gift and favor. They recognized his demise as the necessary outcome of the suffering he had inflicted, and yet they wept for him.

"Truly, no one who persecutes the innocent can thrive," they wailed, shedding copious tears.

Ever debonair, the boy consoled the gentle ladies of the king's court.

Traditional funeral rites were arranged for the king, who would be properly honored in death as he had been in life.

Then, the boy bowed down to the crowd that chanted his name, they who rejoiced in his presence and awakened to his divinity.

Hare Krishna Hare Krishna
Krishna Krishna Hare Hare
Hare Rama Hare Rama
Rama Rama Hare Hare

You May Also Enjoy...

Bhagavad Gita: The Lord's Song
Swamini Sri Lalitambika Devi, Translator
ISBN 978-0-9960236-6-5
Mahakailasa Ashram, 2015

Petals at Your Feet
Swamini Sri Lalitambika Devi, Translator
ISBN 978-0-9960236-3-4
Chintamani Books, 2016

Lalitamba
Edited by Shyam Mukunda
ISSN 1930-0662
Chintamani Books, Annual